Black & White

Abstract

Dedicated for W.K.

Copyright©2014 by Simone Kaplan

Coverpicture ©14 by Simone Kaplan

All rights reserved by Simone Kaplan

Old Filling Station

This old filling station did not operate any more. It was fenced in and it looked like a museum piece with the strange winding elastic tubes and metal pipes. For me this was of course a paradise.I love abstract forms and lines.
Nevertheless, here I had really found a goldmine.
A look at the sun.... she sent her soft, gentle morning rays exactly on the old filling station. The strangest forms and figures thereby arose.
Oh I was so happy at this moment. Also the metal of the fence shone in the sun like silver.
I knelt on the ground and took pictures off.... the surroundings I had completely forgotten.

Suddenly a voice sounded behind me...
„Hey what do you make there??"
I looked up frightened and.... directly in a questioning face. It was the tenant to whom this old filling station belonged.
When she saw my nervous face, a smile darted over her face and she indicated questioningly at my camera.
Hesitantly I answered that me only the abstract forms interested in the petrol pumps and tubes.
The tenant gave a laugh and the situation relaxed.She told me that it looked strange when she saw from the window, somebody on the knees before the fence.

Here the result of my efforts on the knees :)

Simone Kaplan Black & White: Abstract

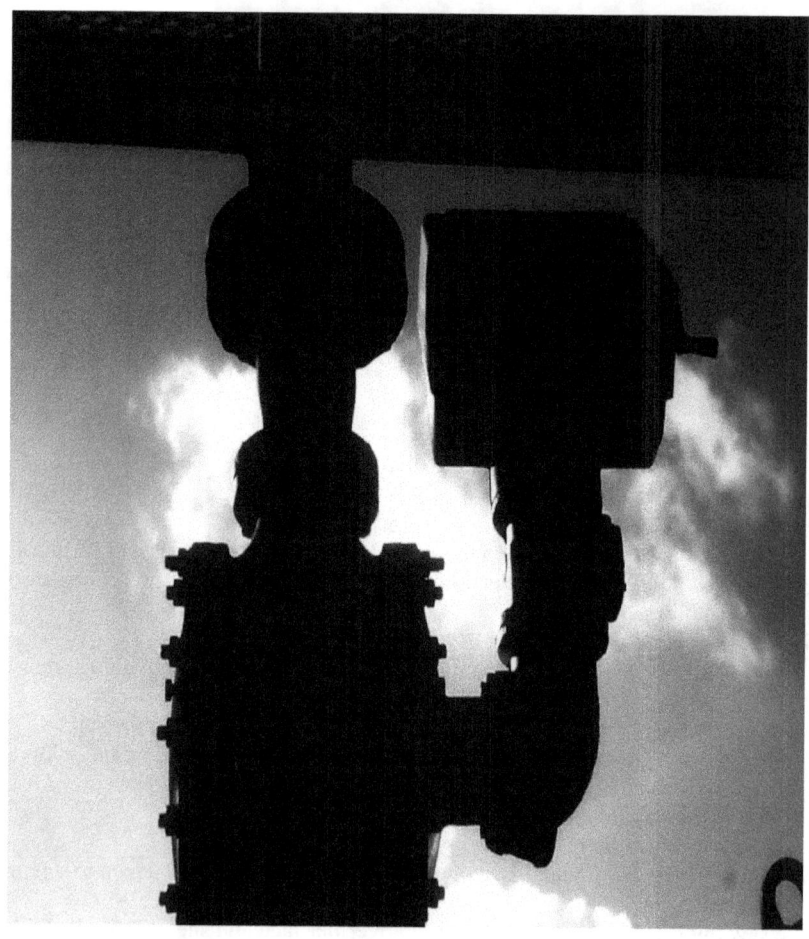

Simone Kaplan   Black & White: Abstract

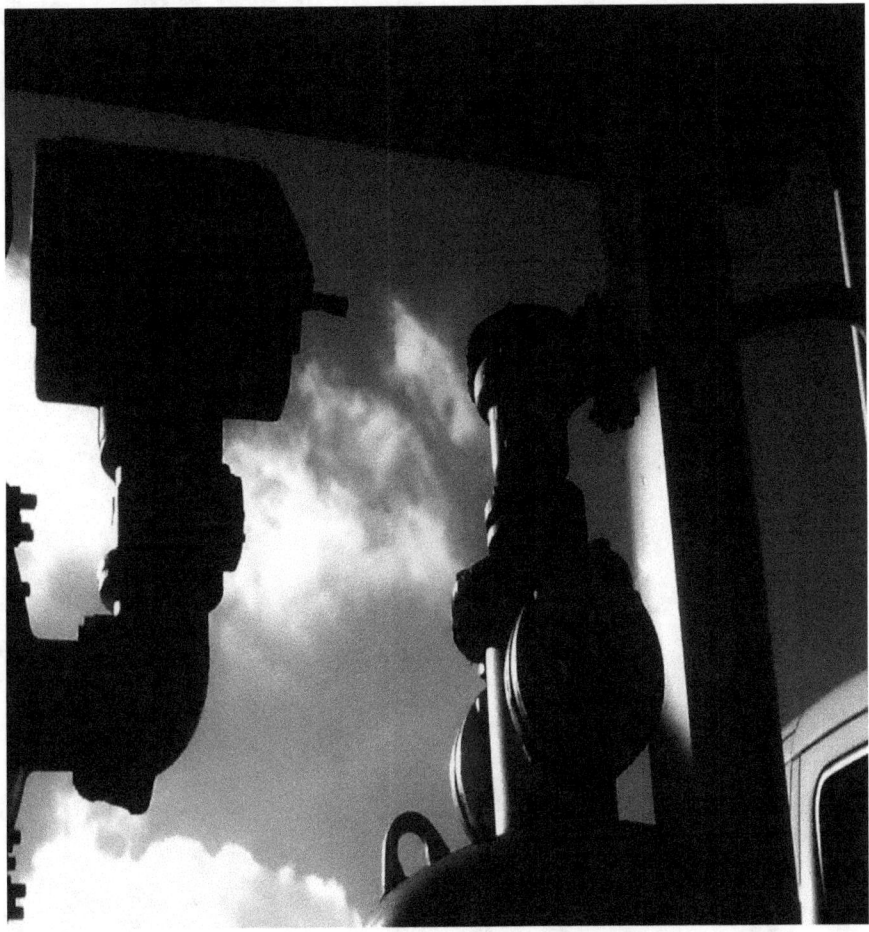

Simone Kaplan   Black & White: Abstract

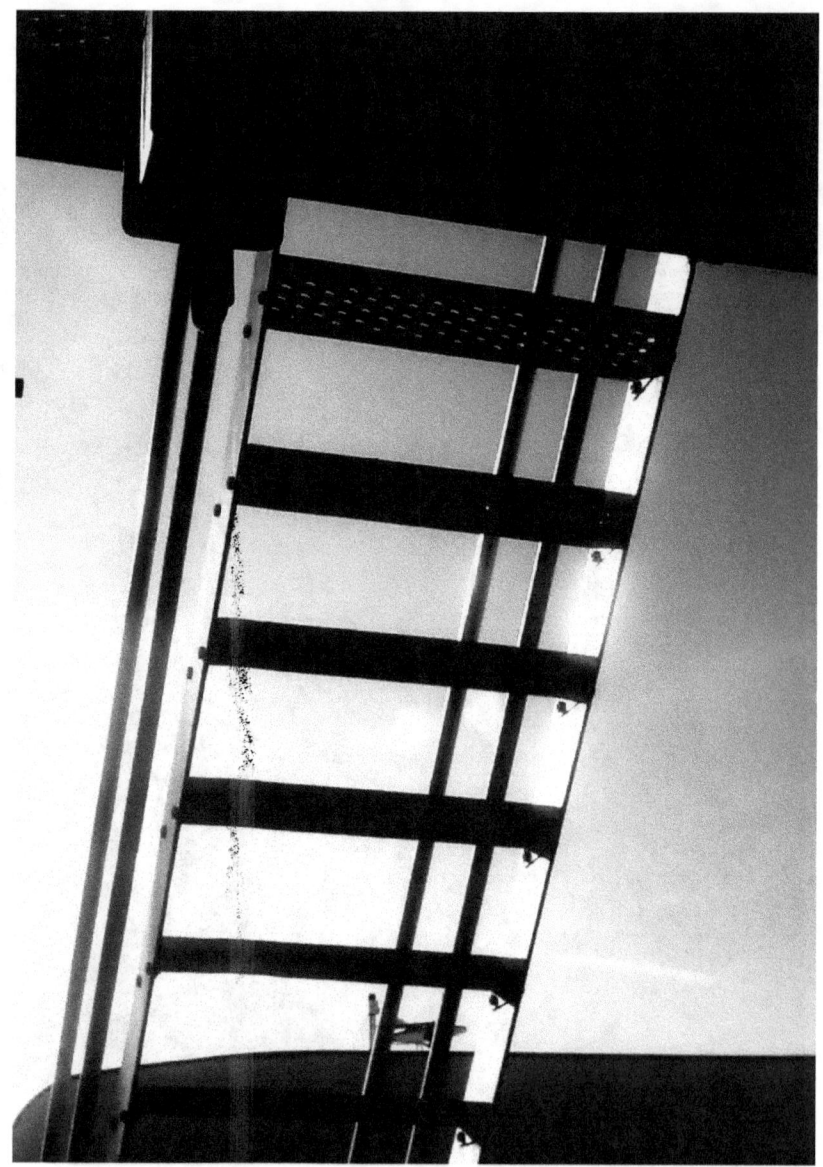

Simone Kaplan
Black & White: Abstract

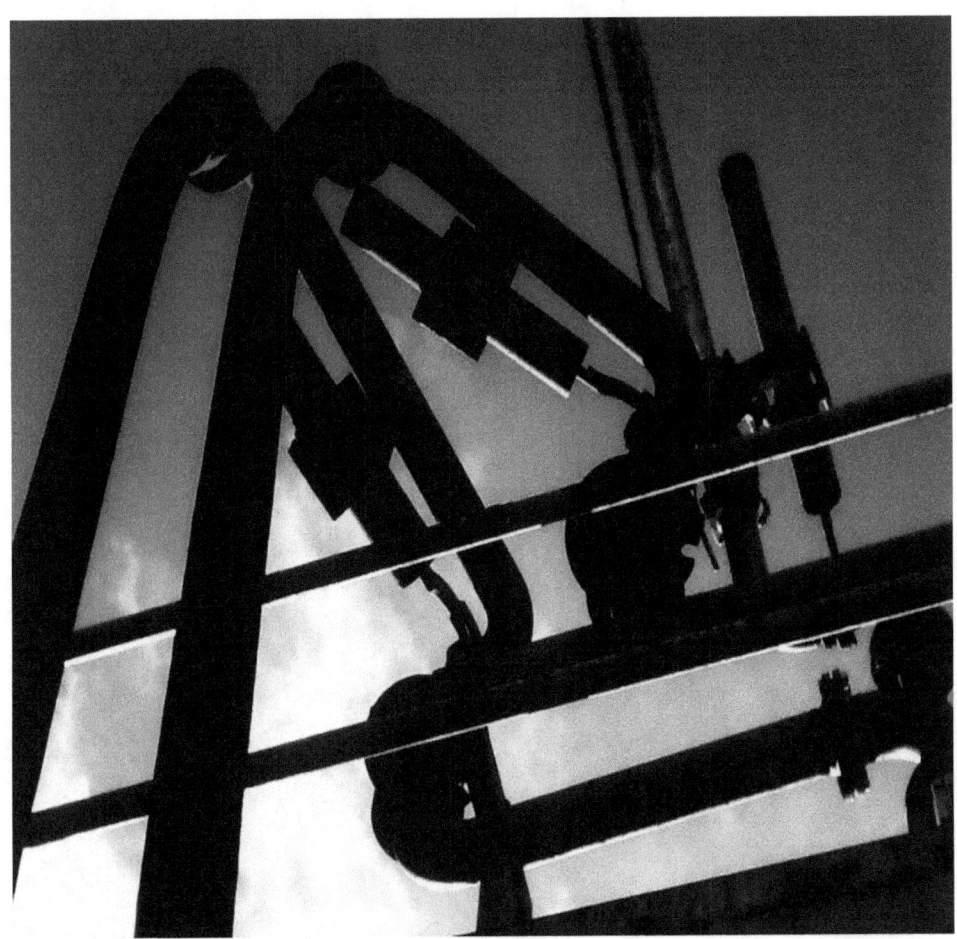

Simone Kaplan   Black & White: Abstract

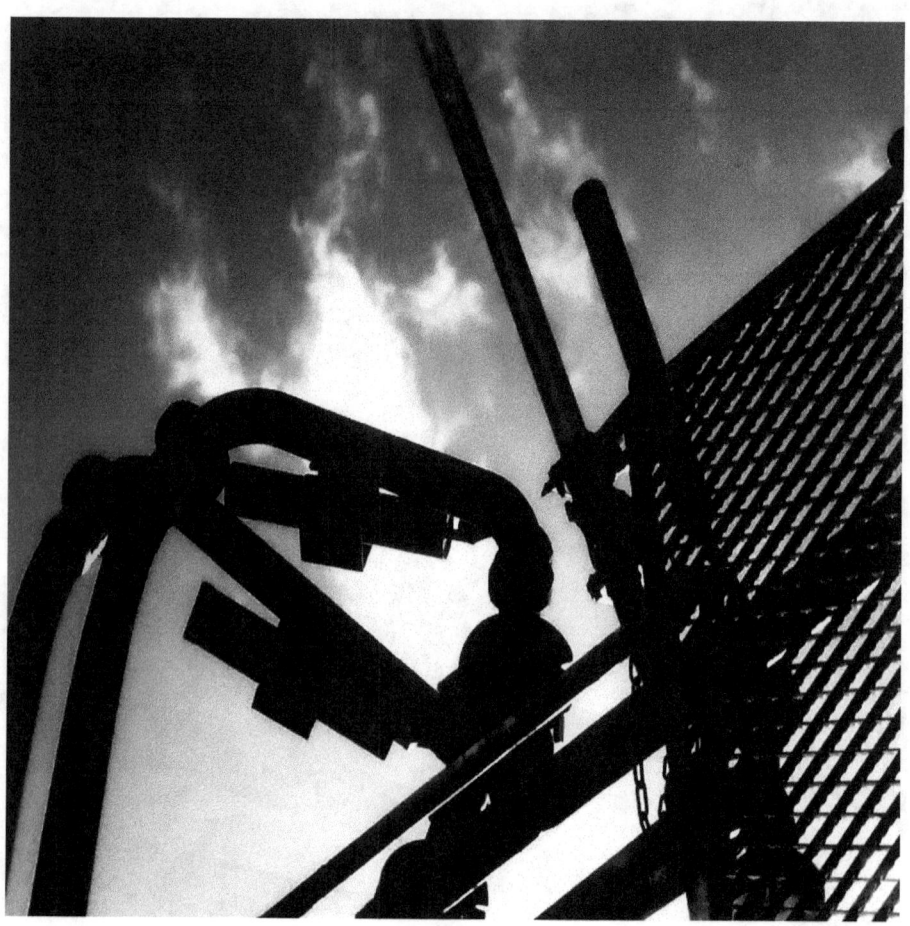

Simone Kaplan Black & White: Abstract

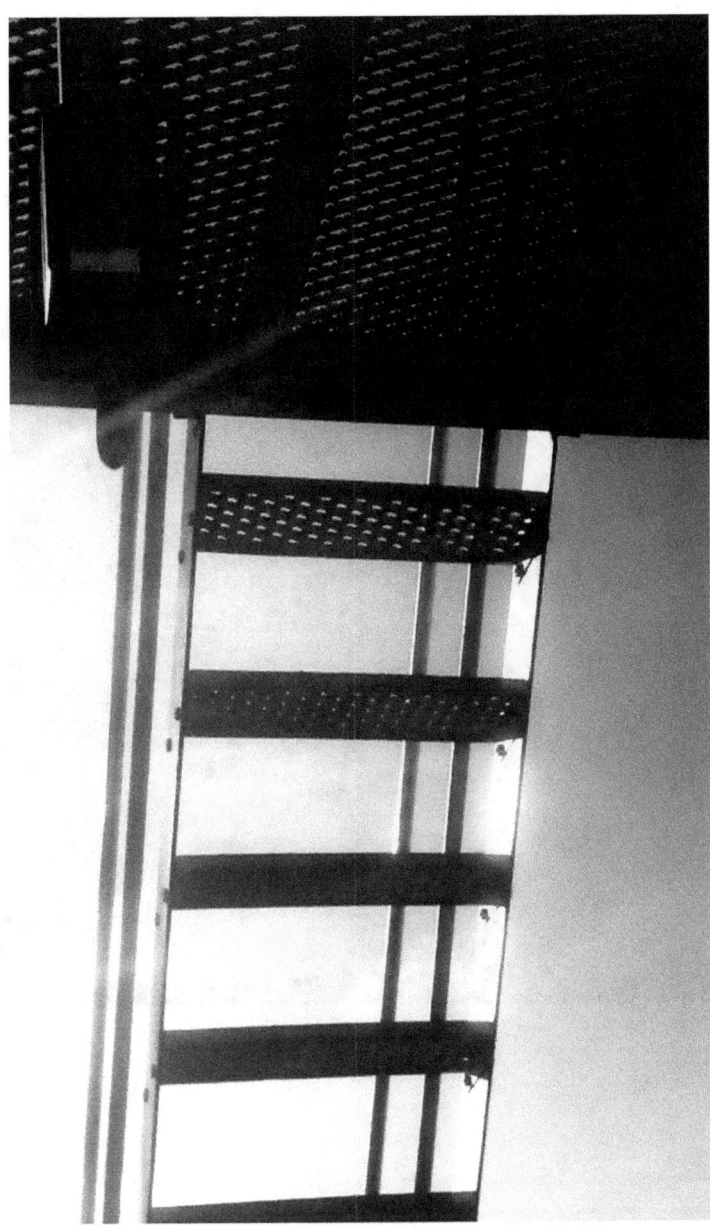

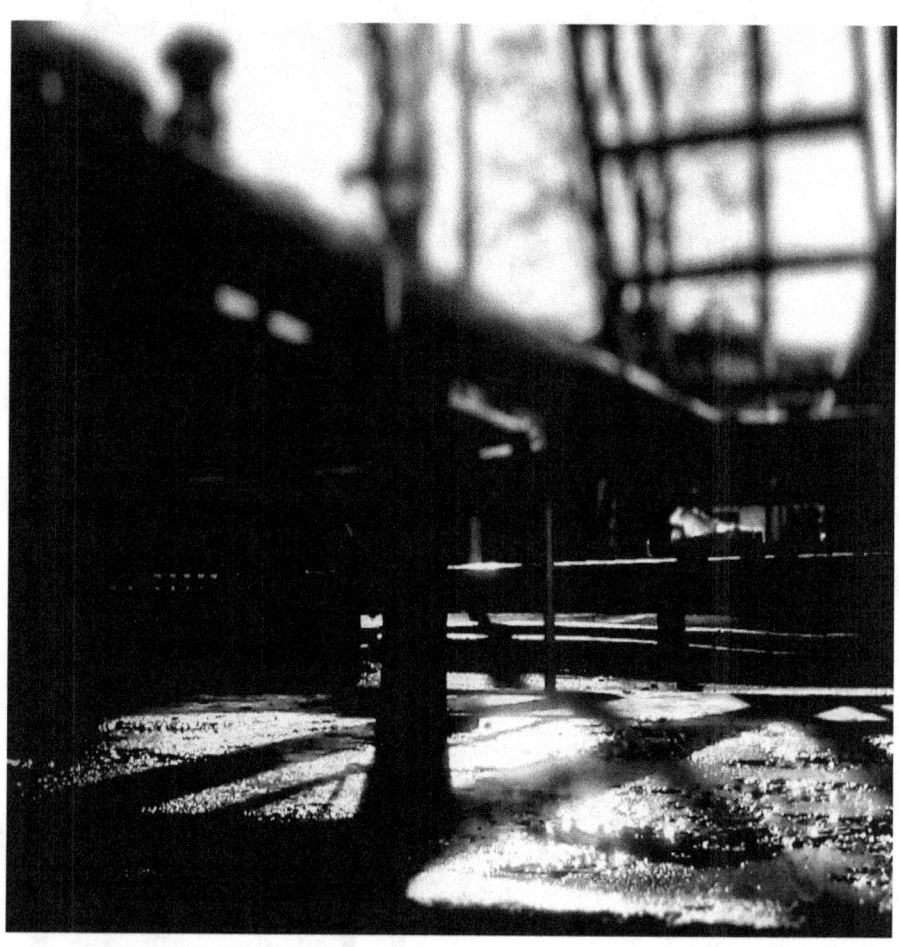

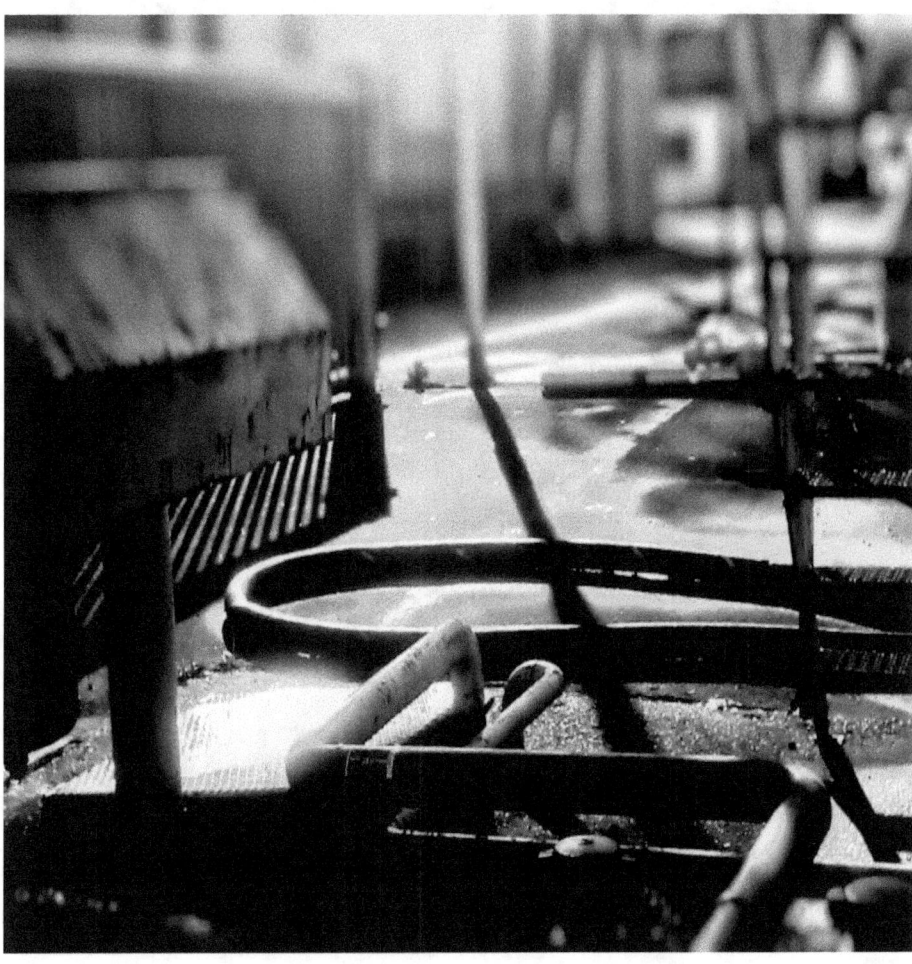

Simone Kaplan Black & White: Abstract

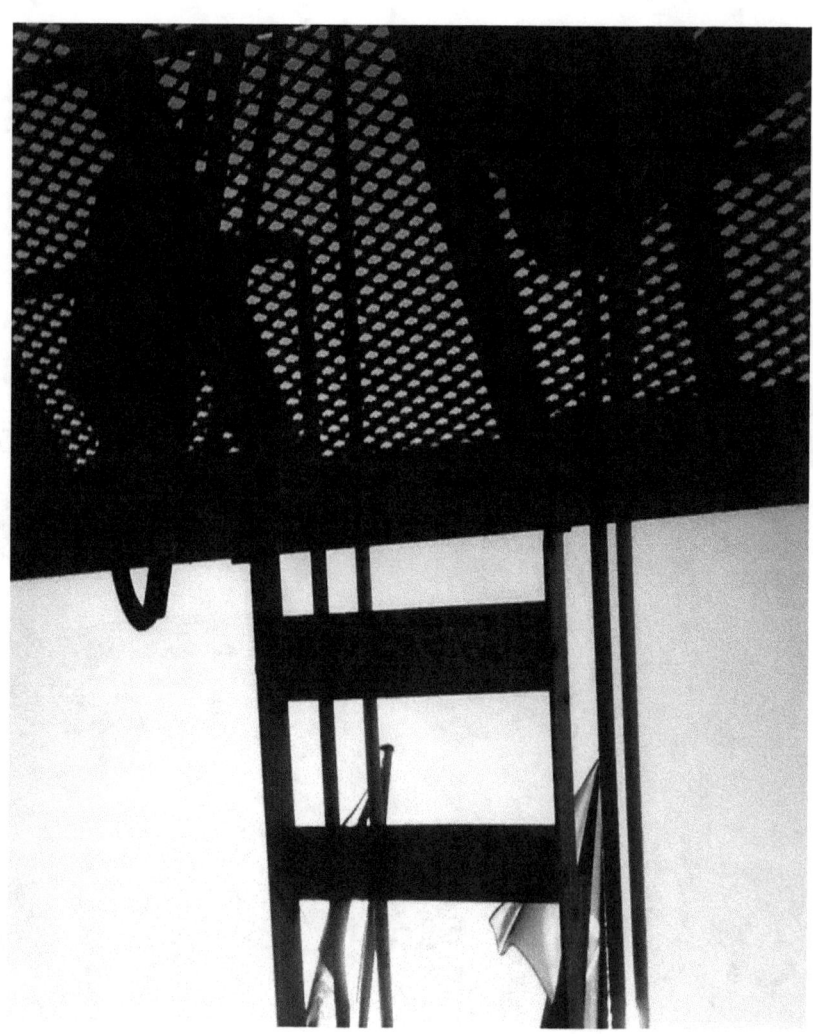

Simone Kaplan   Black & White: Abstract

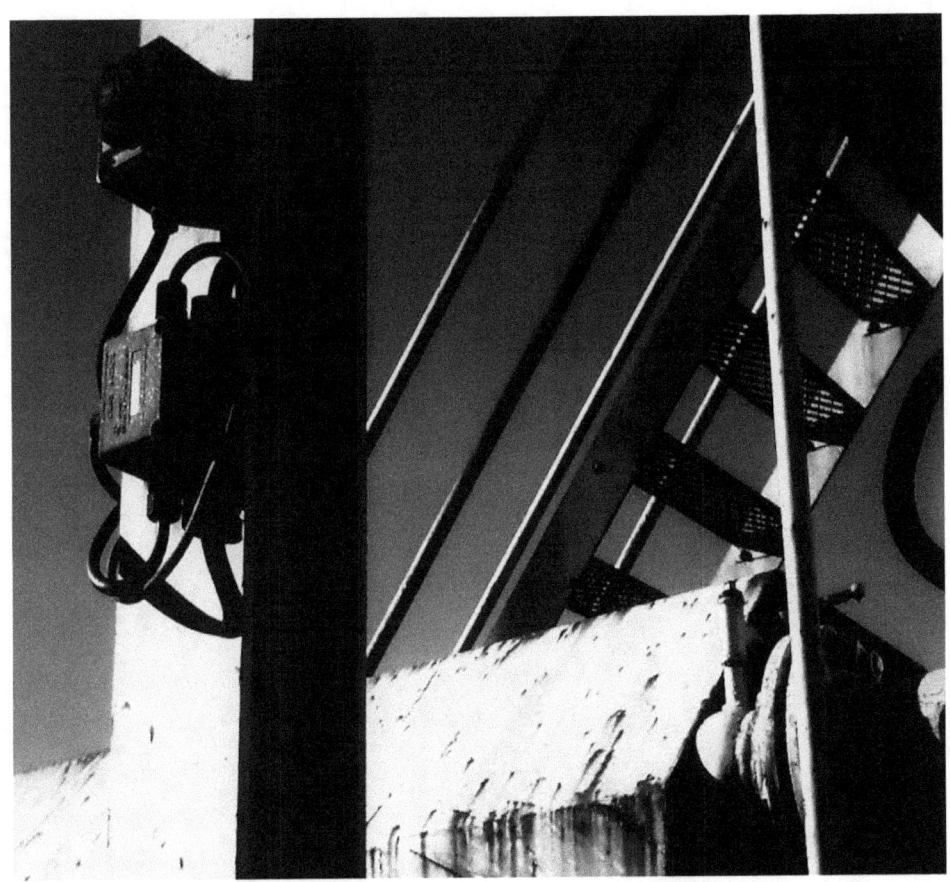

Simone Kaplan   Black & White: Abstract

Simone Kaplan   Black & White: Abstract

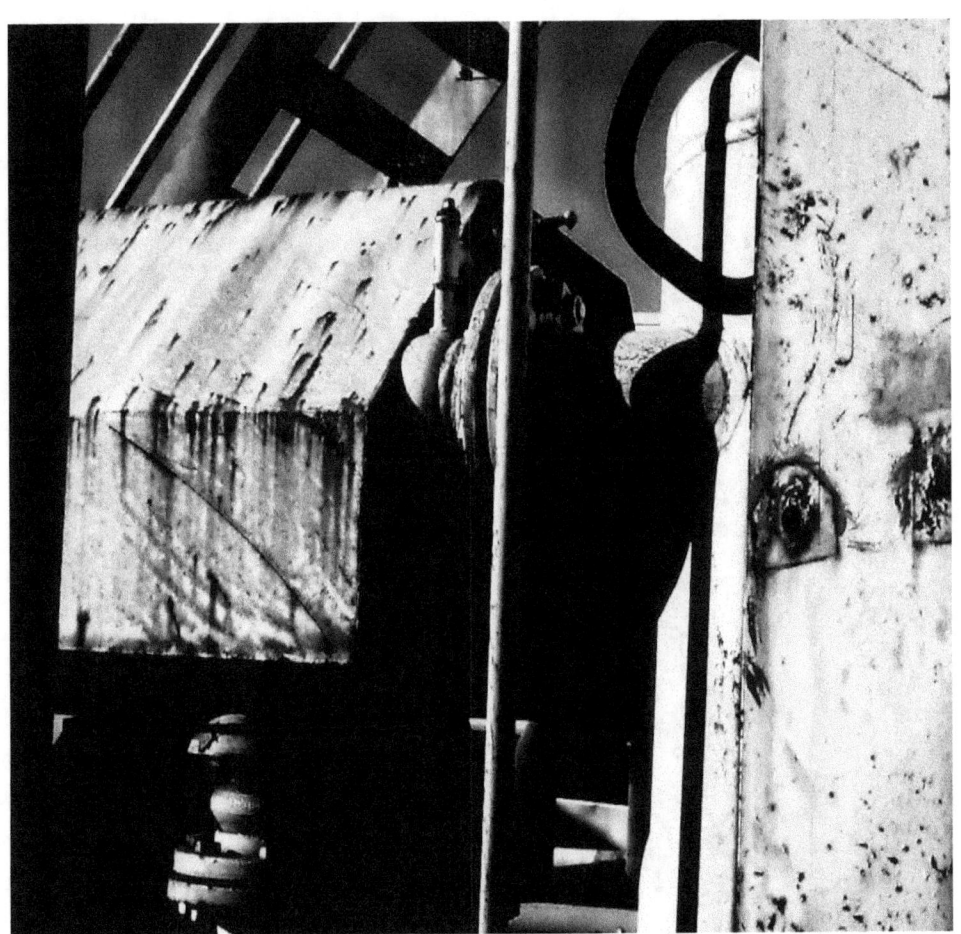

Simone Kaplan   Black & White: Abstract

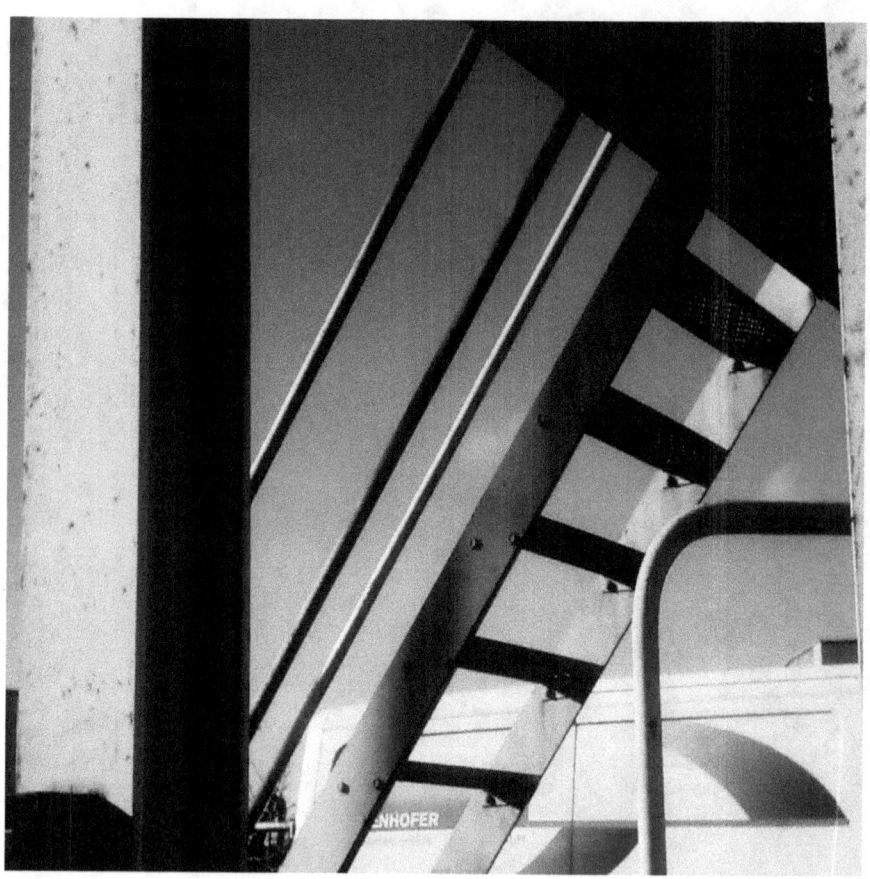

Simone Kaplan Black & White: Abstract

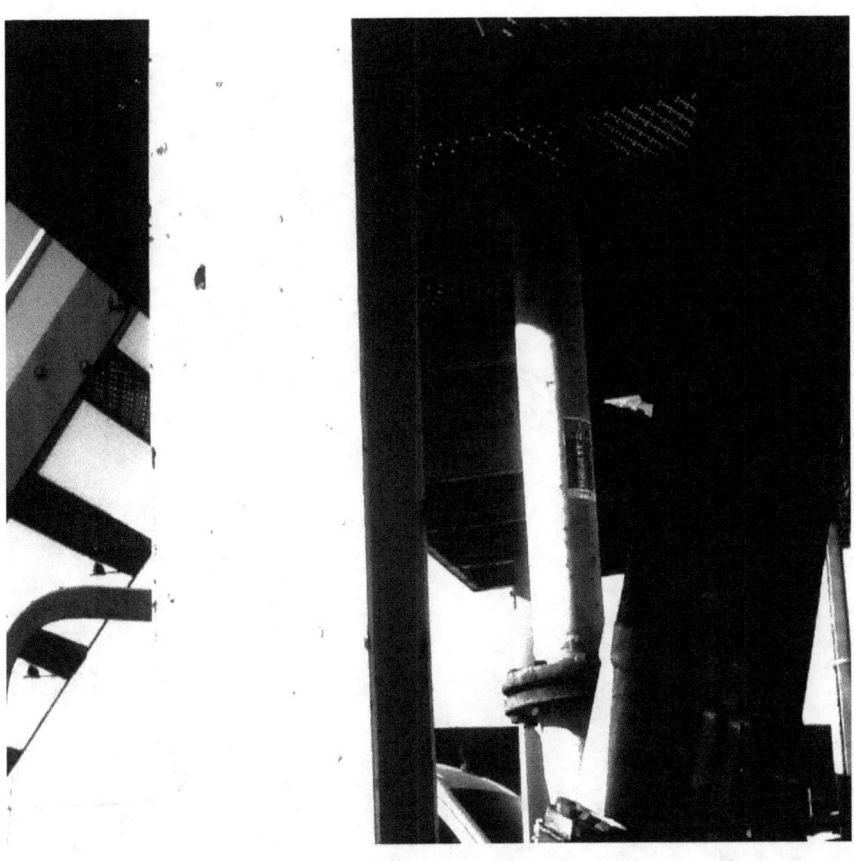

Simone Kaplan   Black & White: Abstract

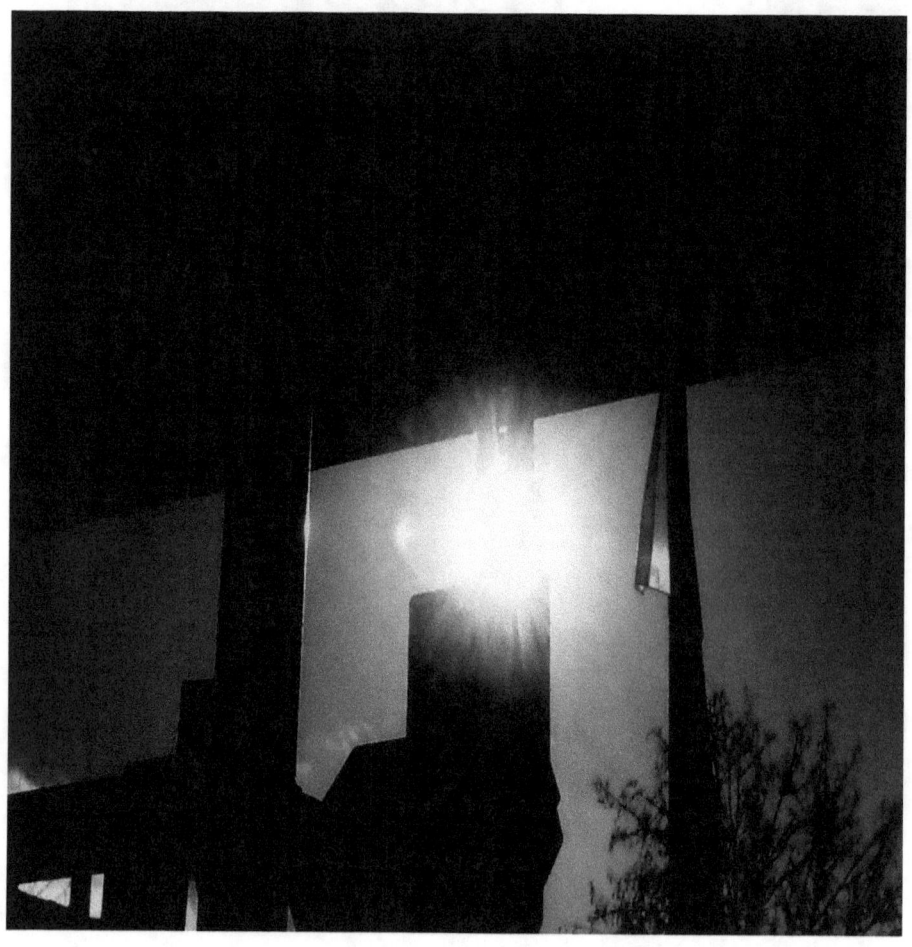

Simone Kaplan   Black & White: Abstract

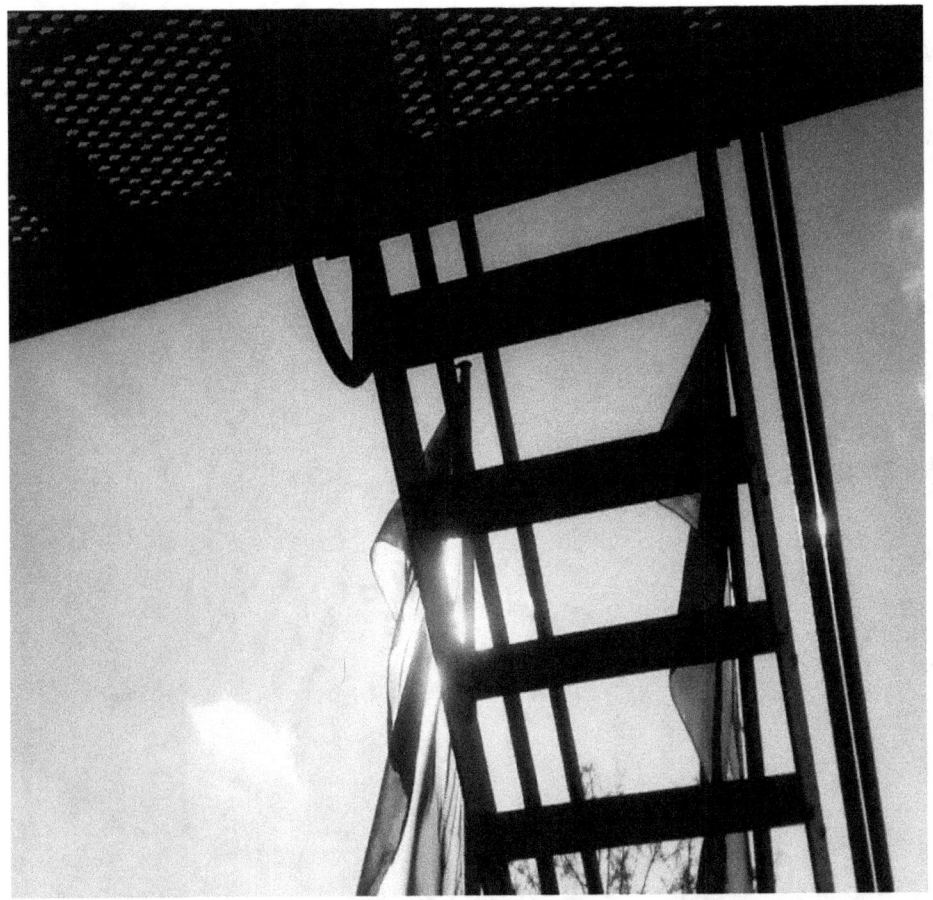

Simone Kaplan Black & White: Abstract

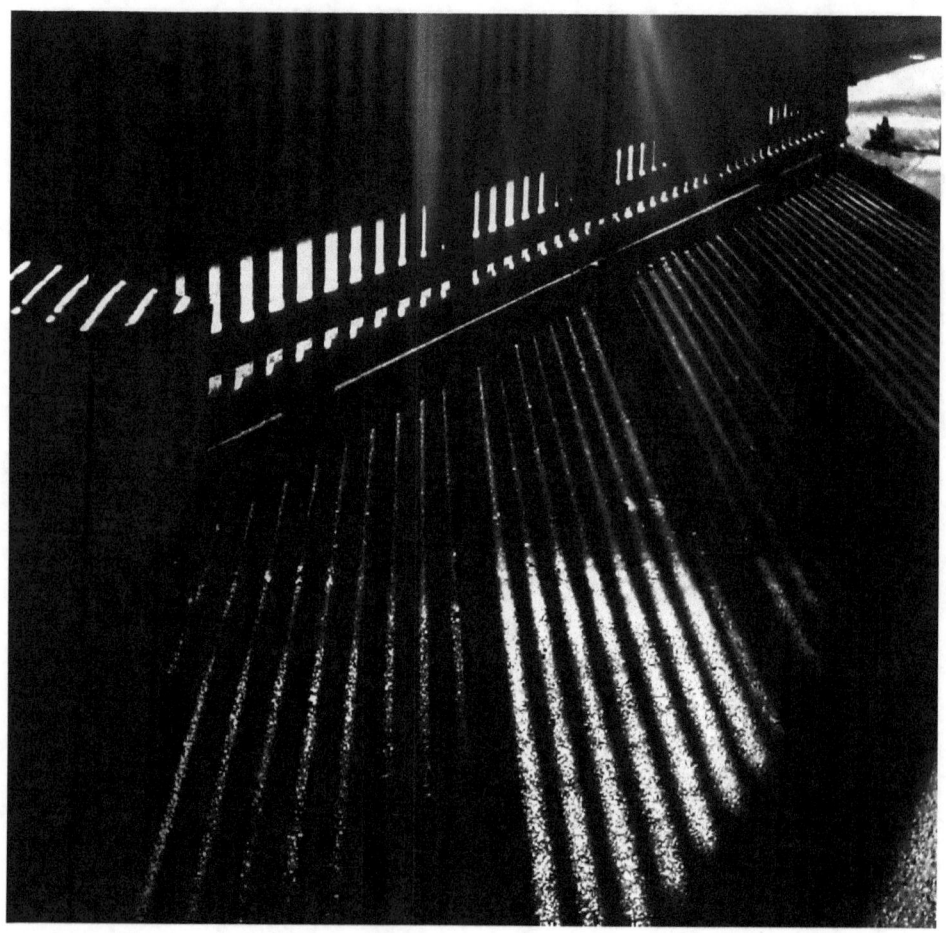

Simone Kaplan   Black & White: Abstract

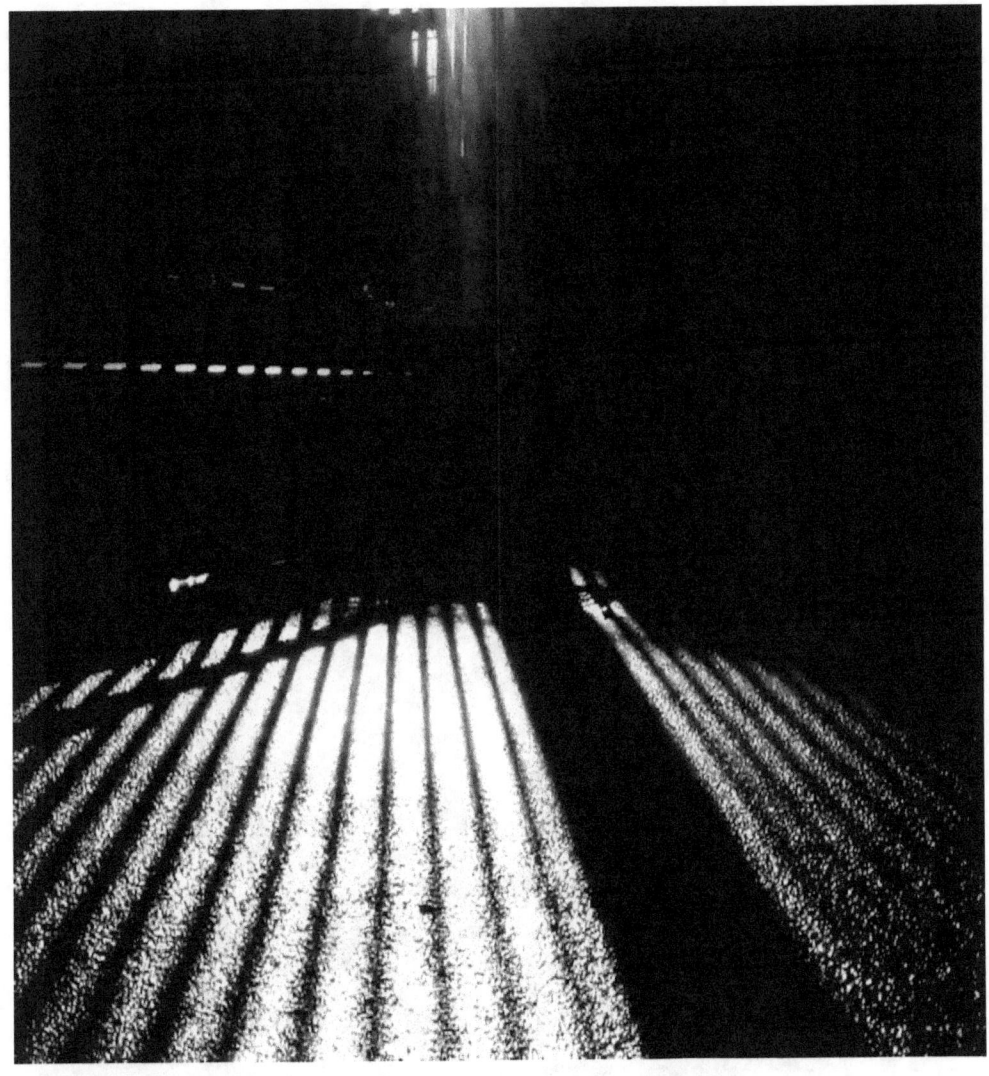

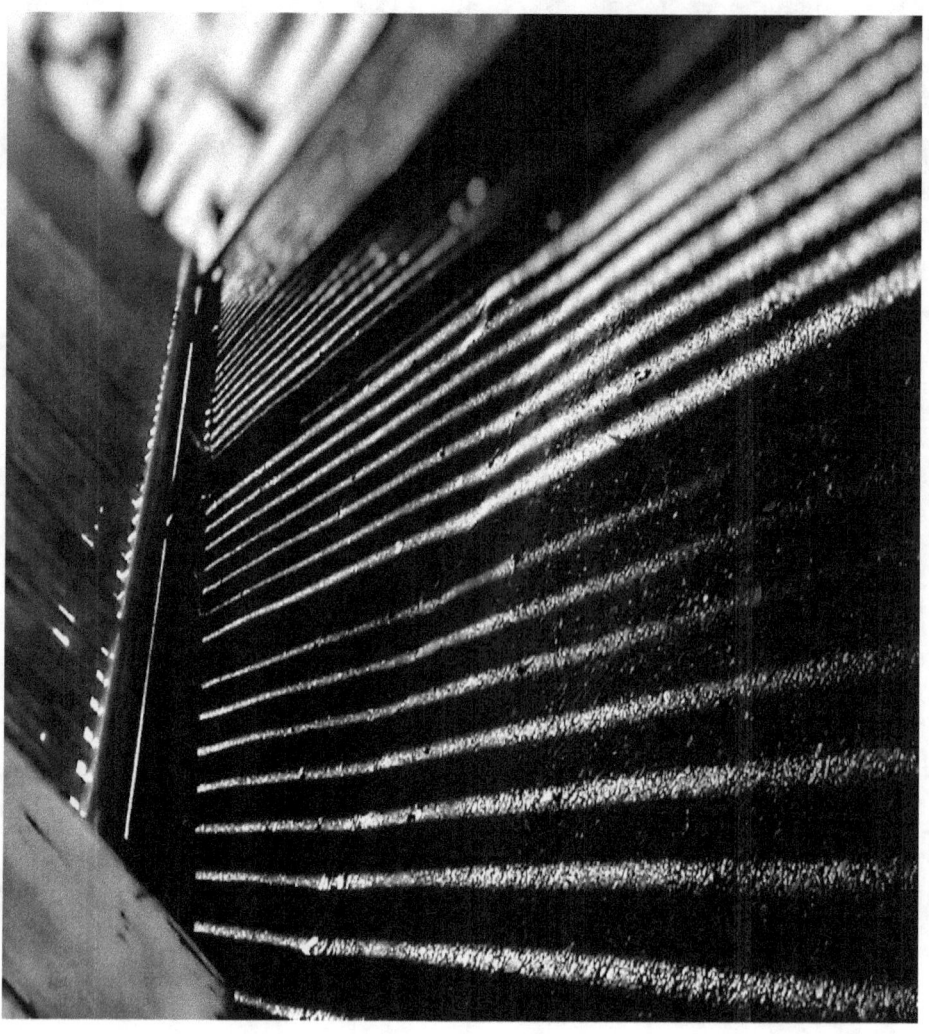

Simone Kaplan   Black & White: Abstract

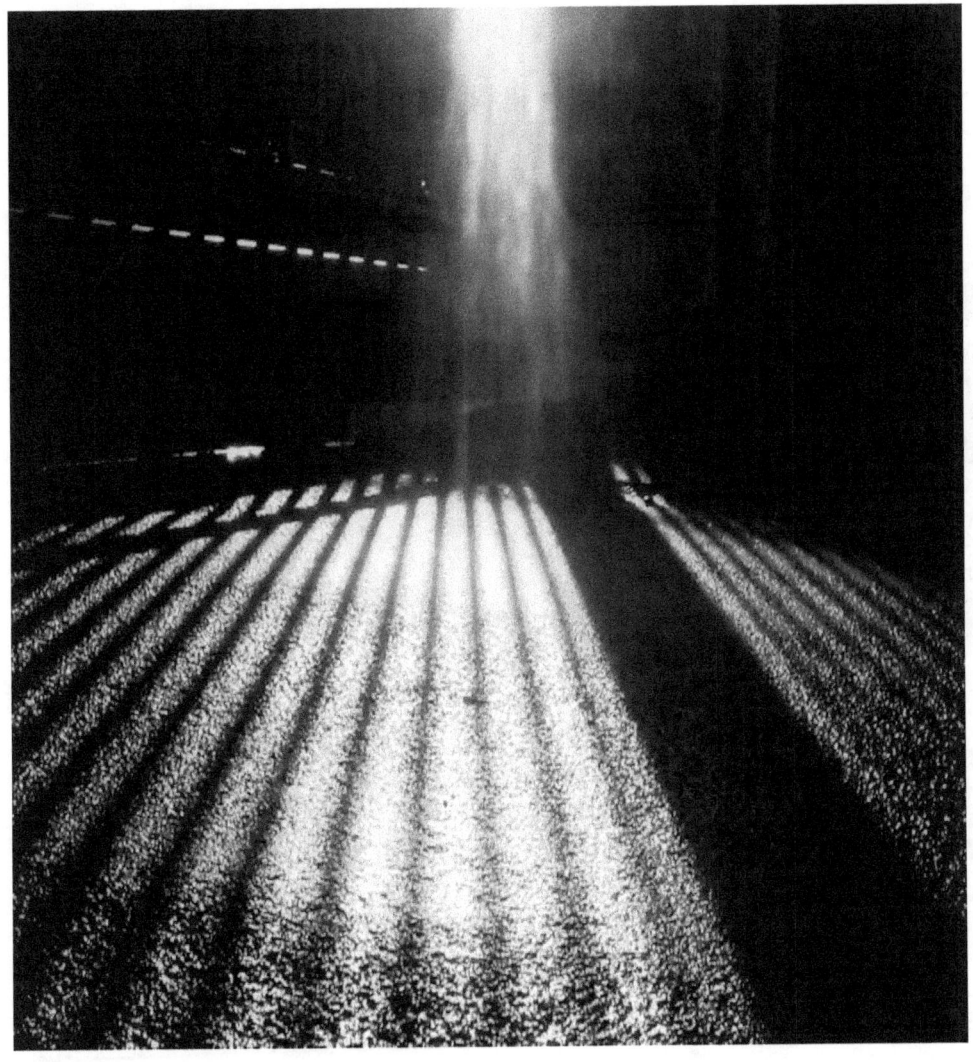

Simone Kaplan　　　　　　　　　　　　　　　　　　　　　　　　　　Black & White: Abstract

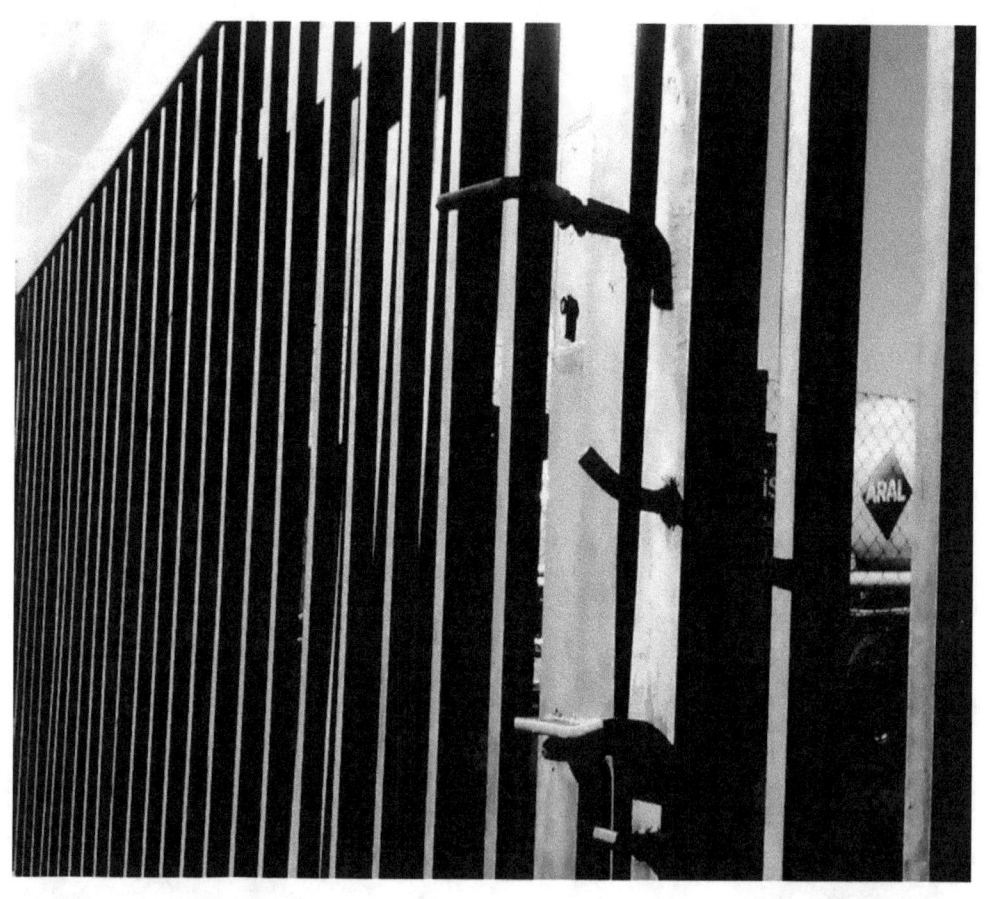

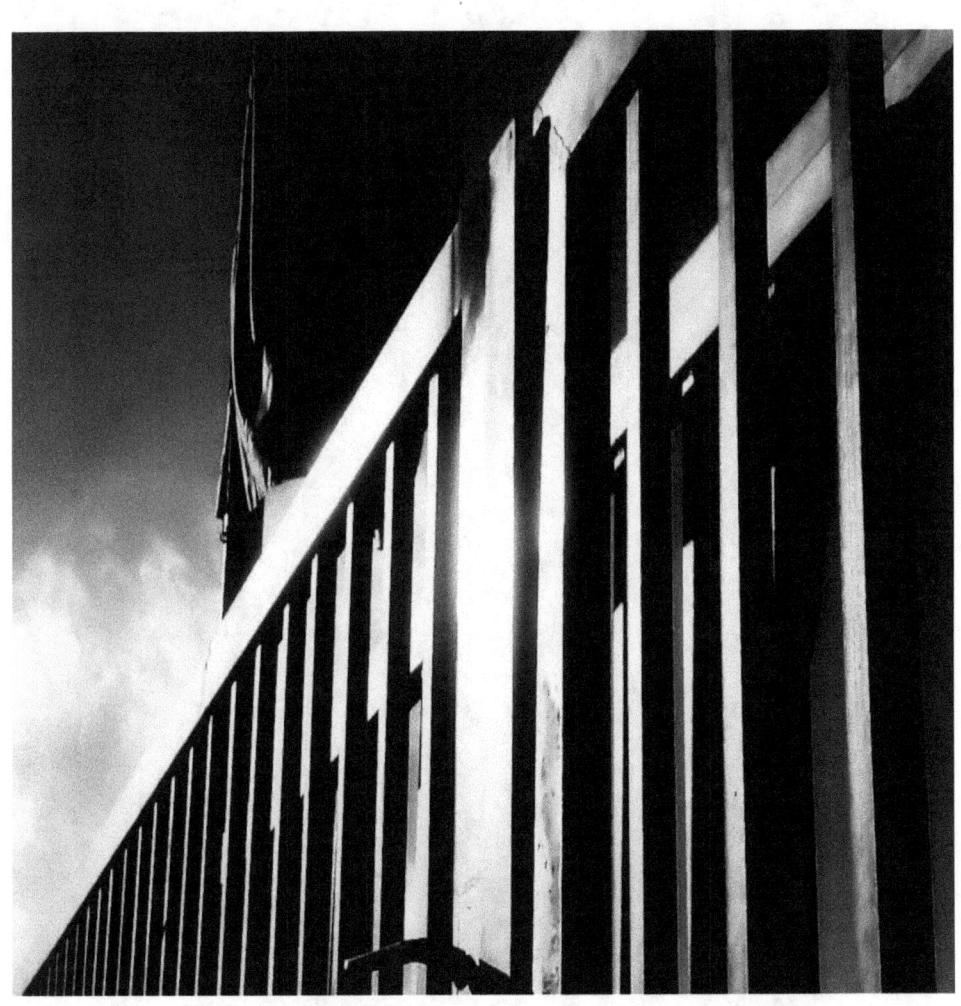

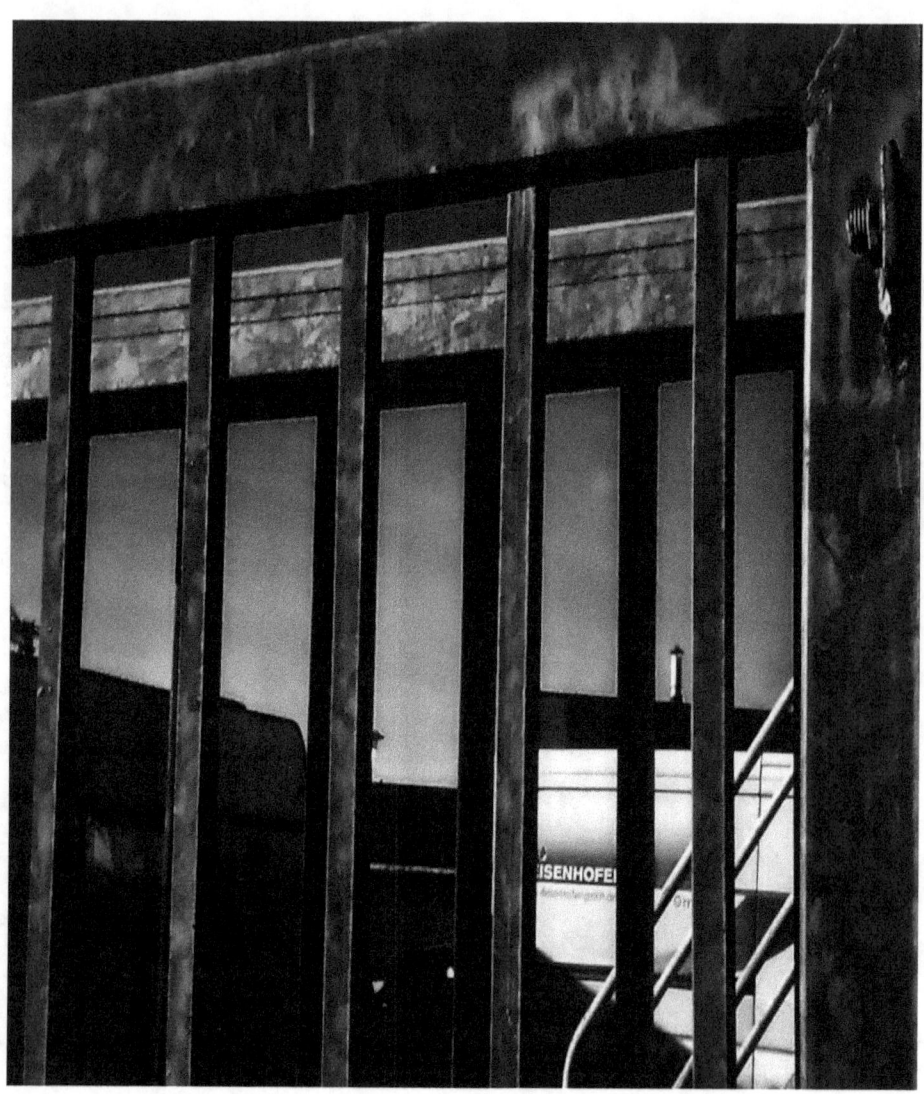

Simone Kaplan Black & White: Abstract

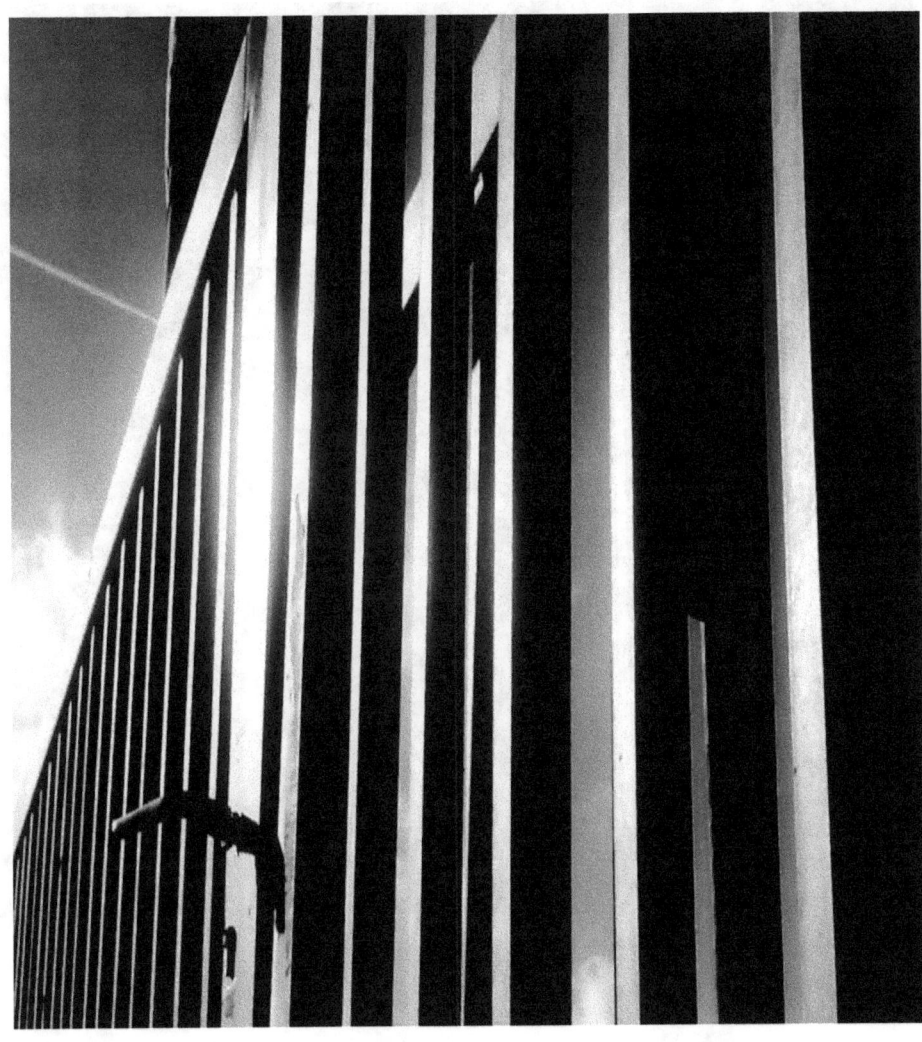

Simone Kaplan Black & White: Abstract

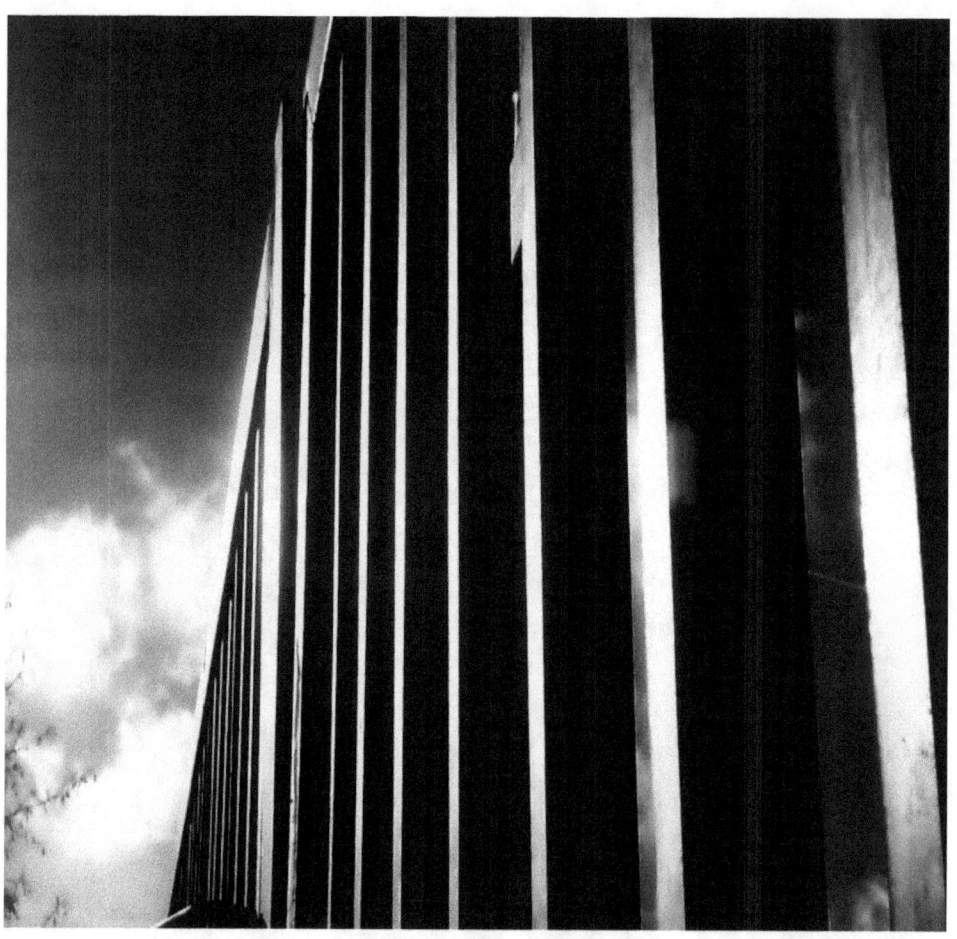

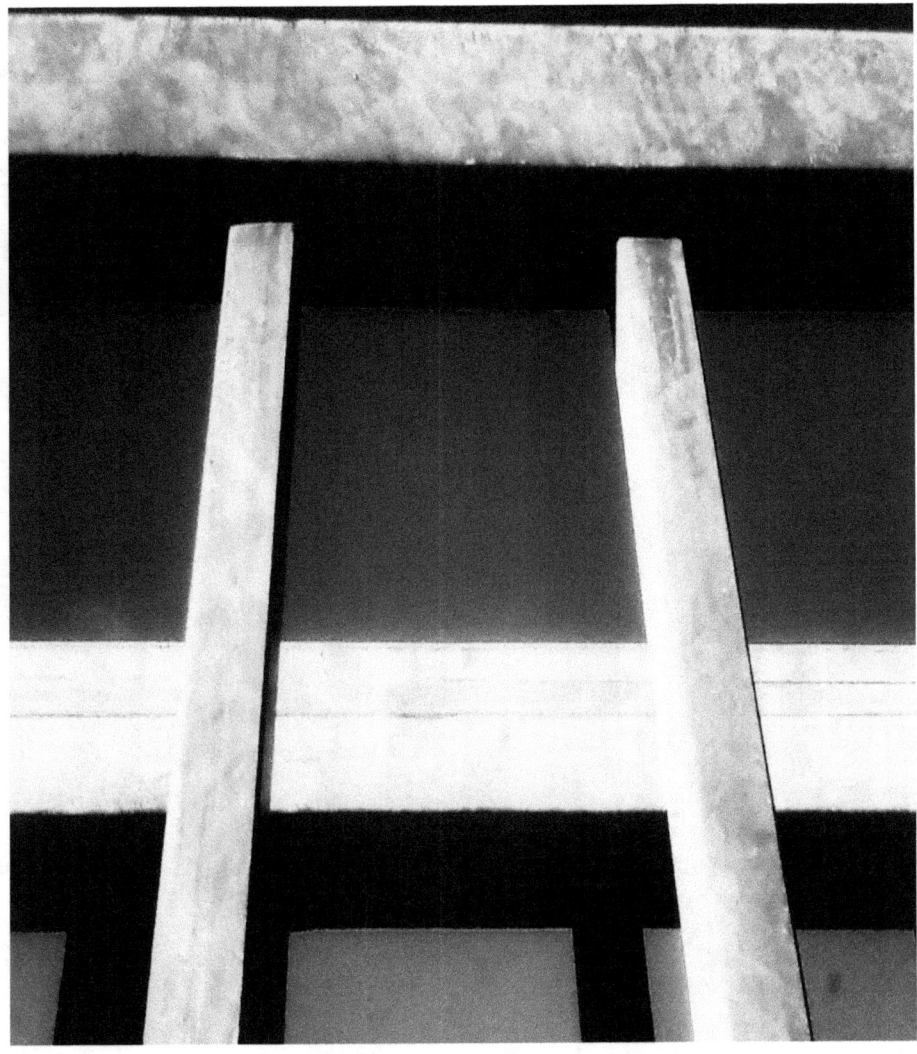

Simone Kaplan   Black & White: Abstract

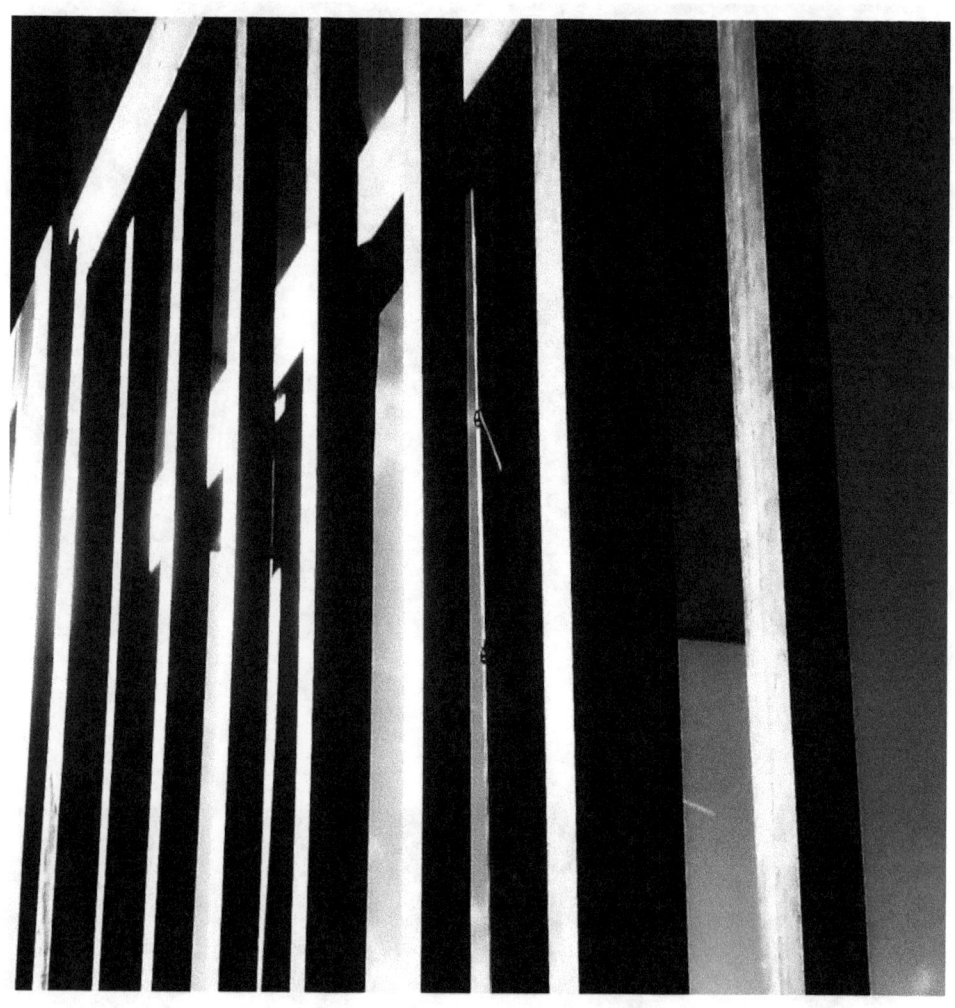

Simone Kaplan   Black & White: Abstract

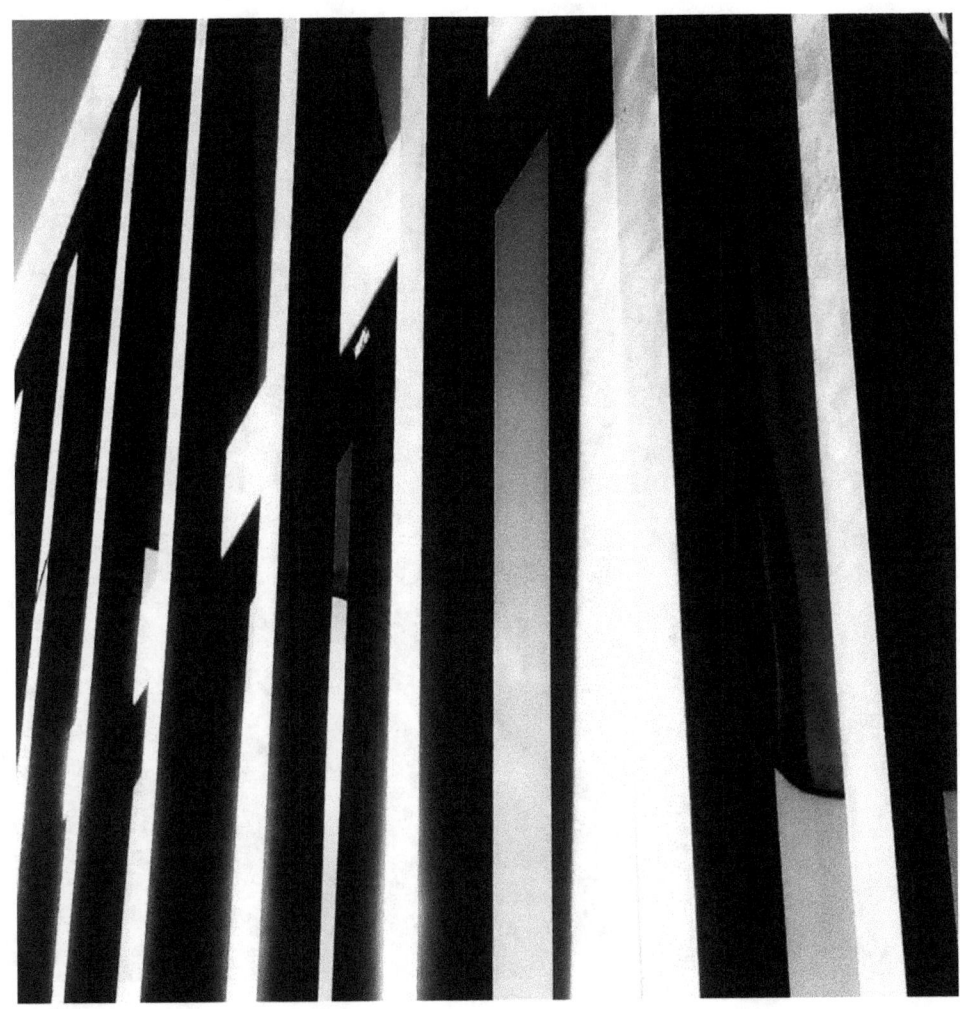

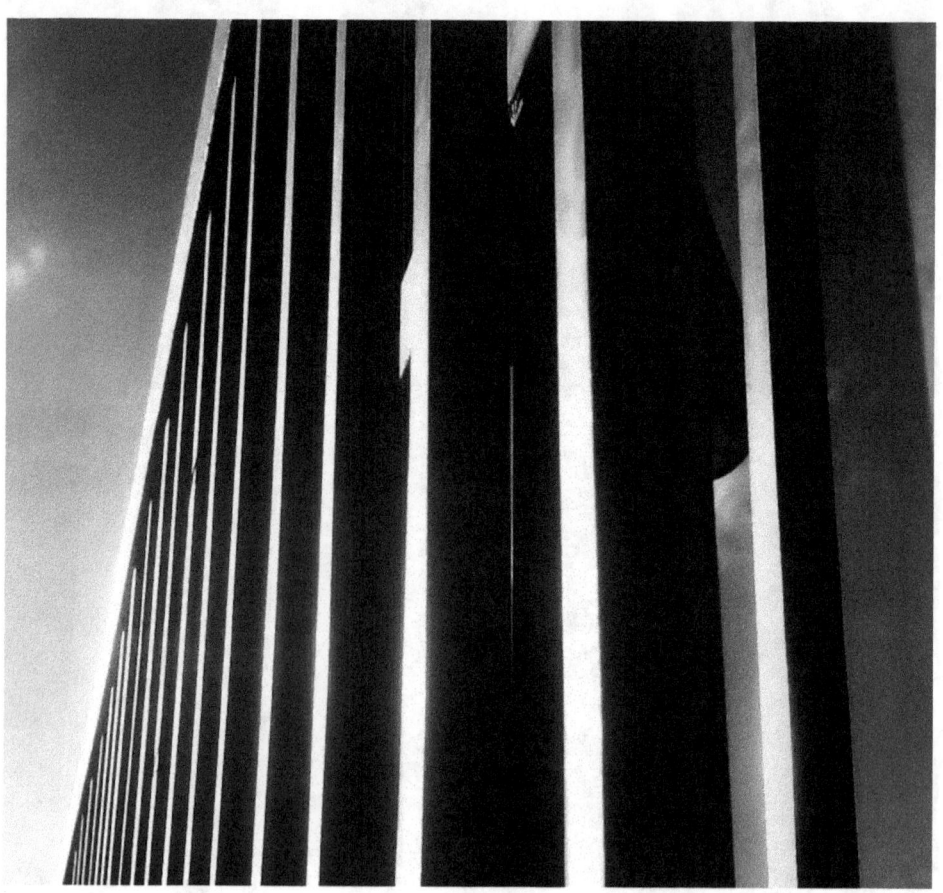

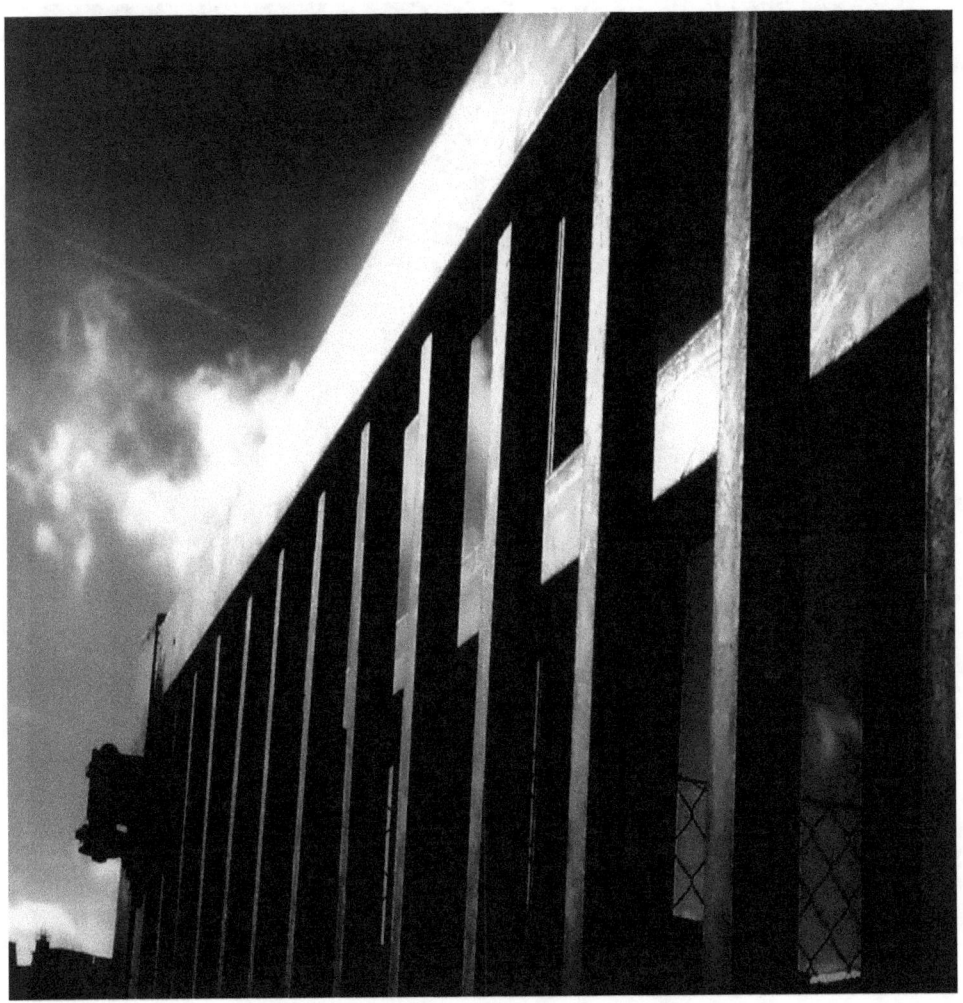

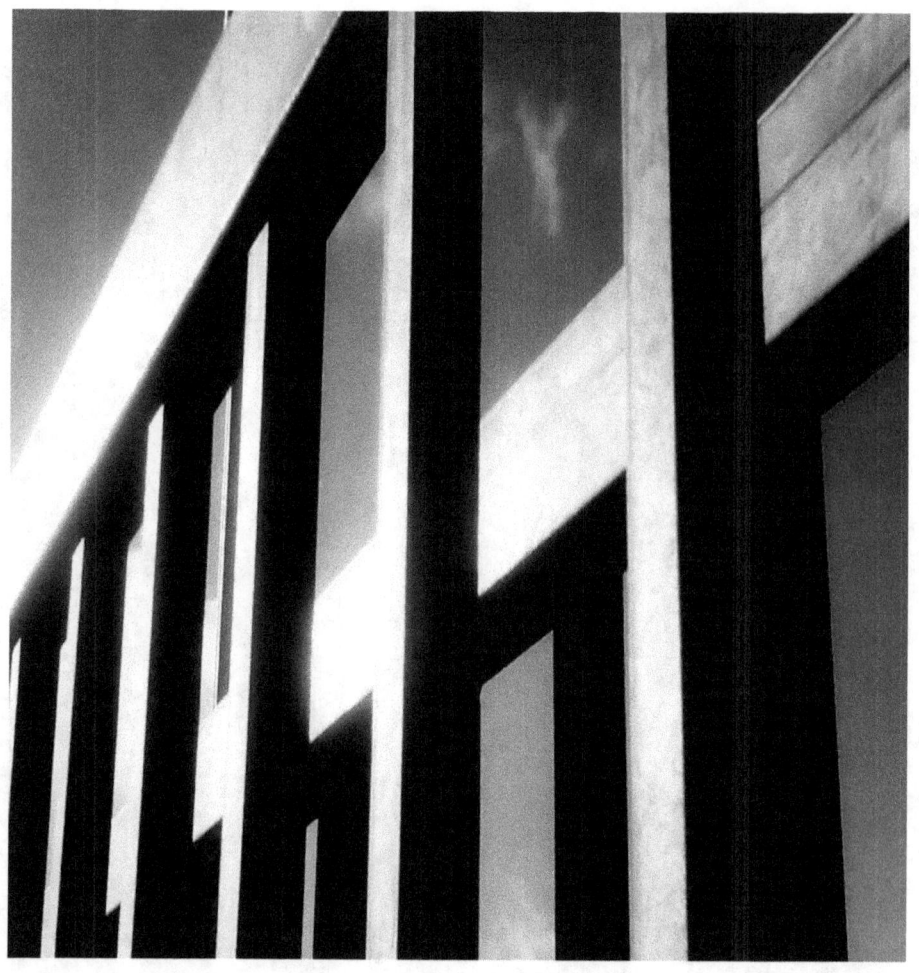

Simone Kaplan — Black & White: Abstract

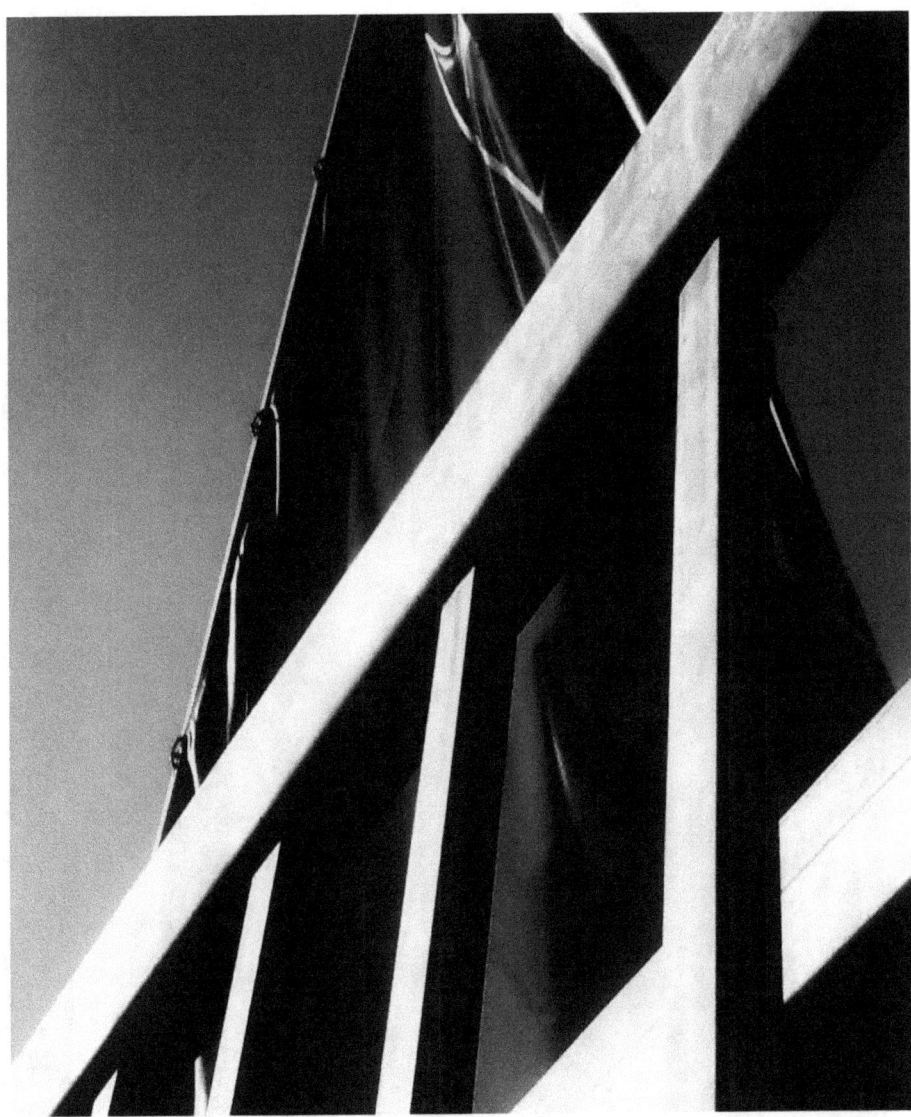

Simone Kaplan Black & White: Abstract

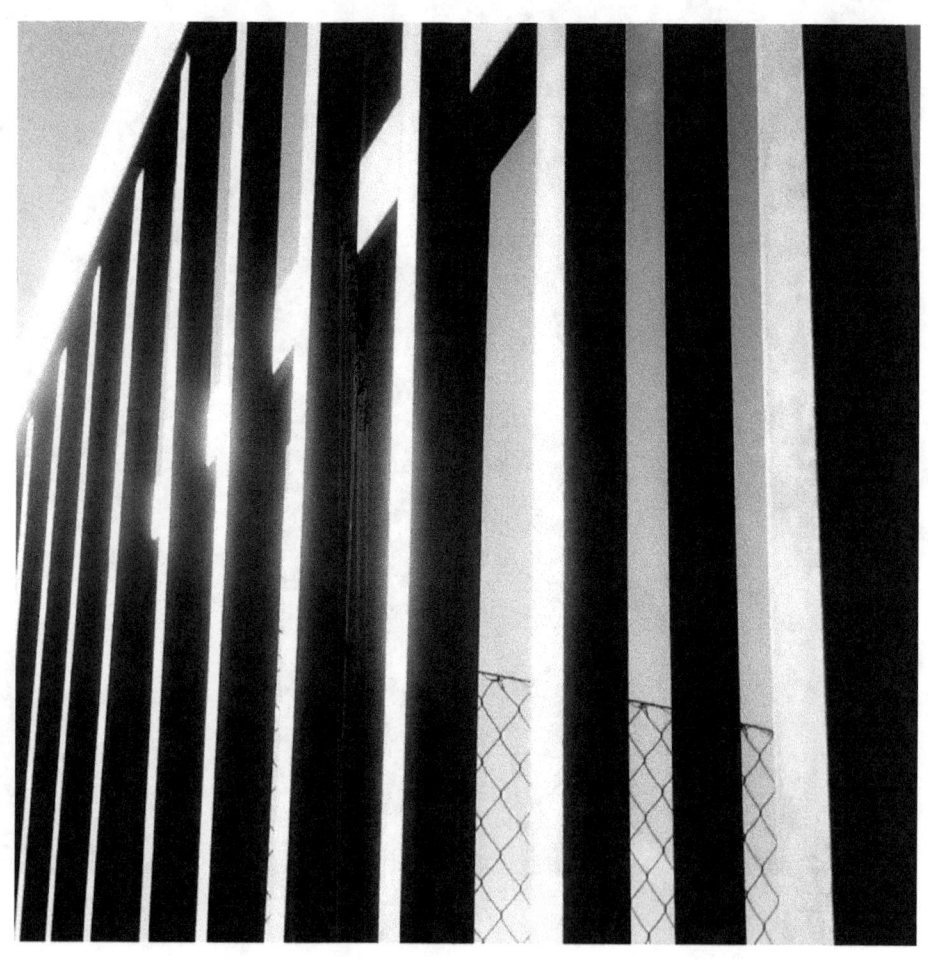

Simone Kaplan					Black & White: Abstract

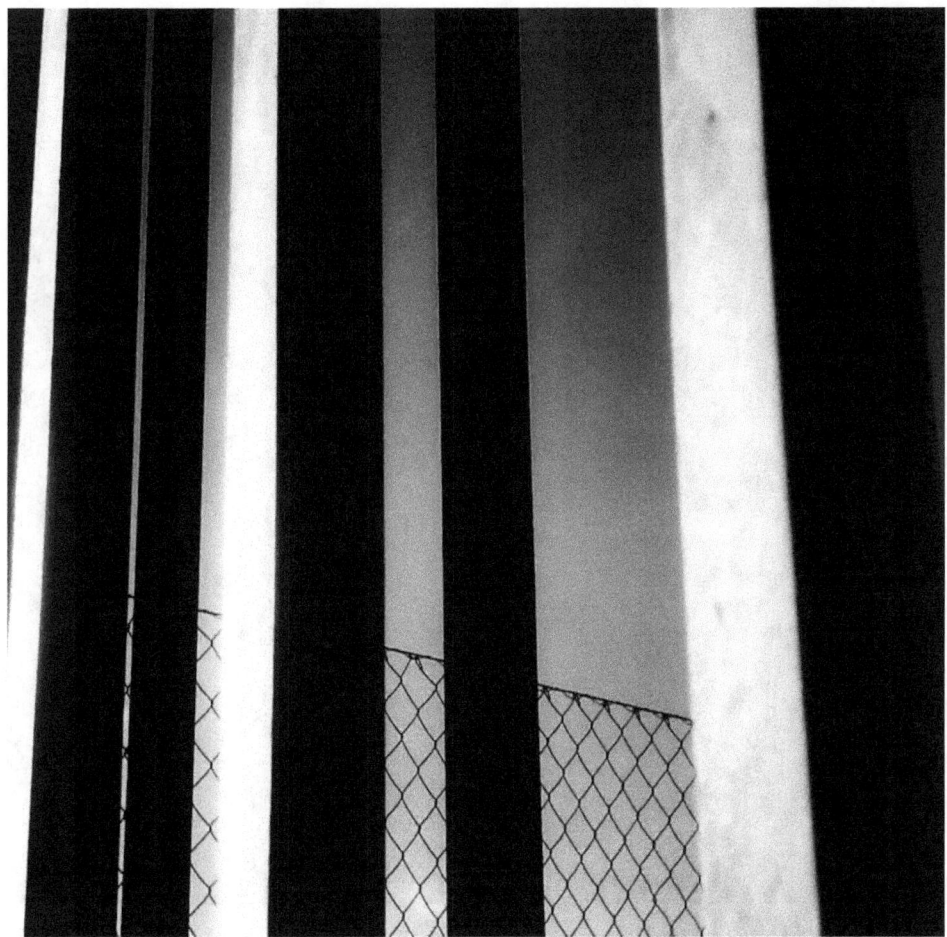

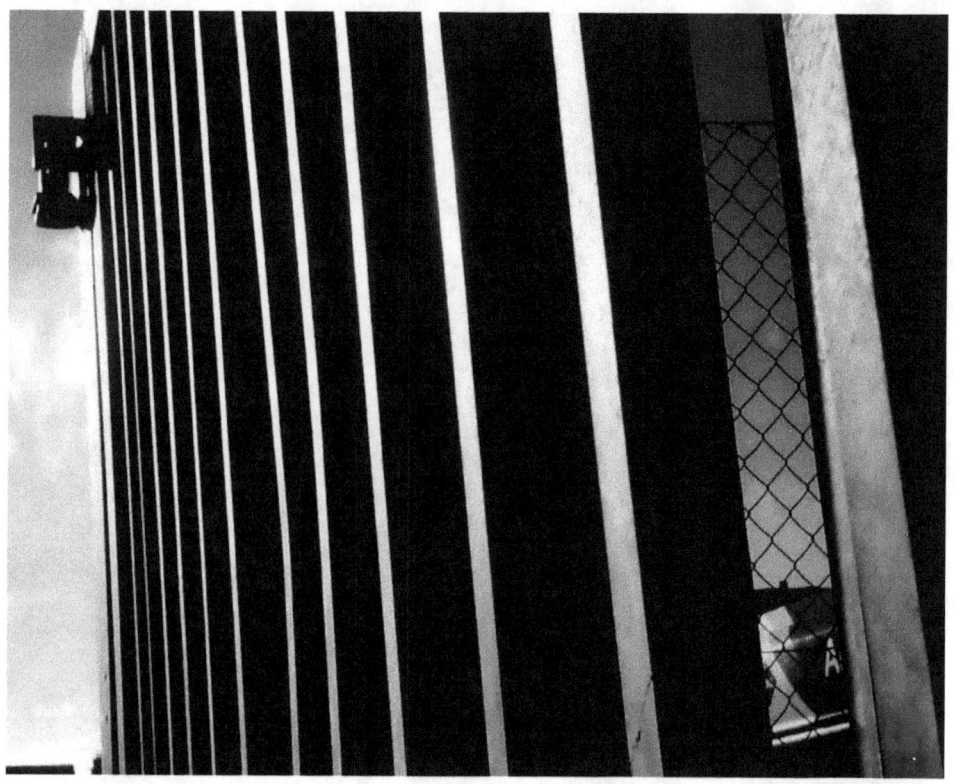

Simone Kaplan   Black & White: Abstract

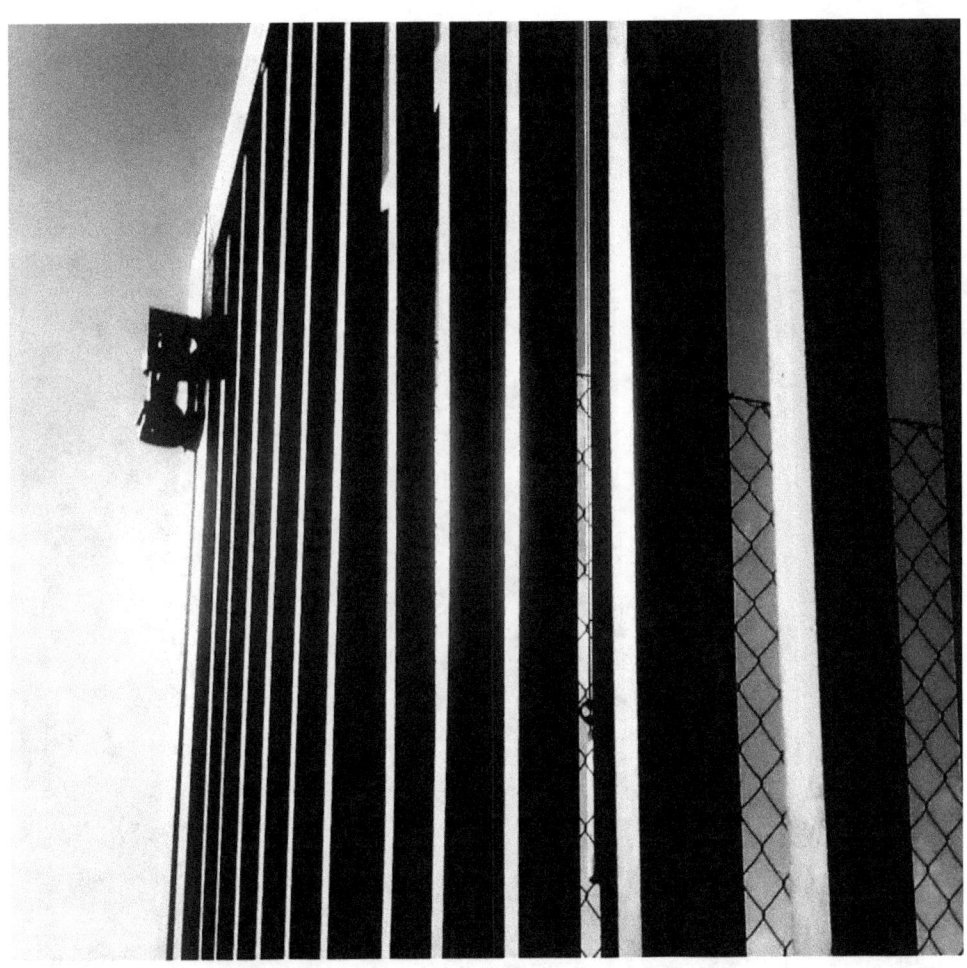

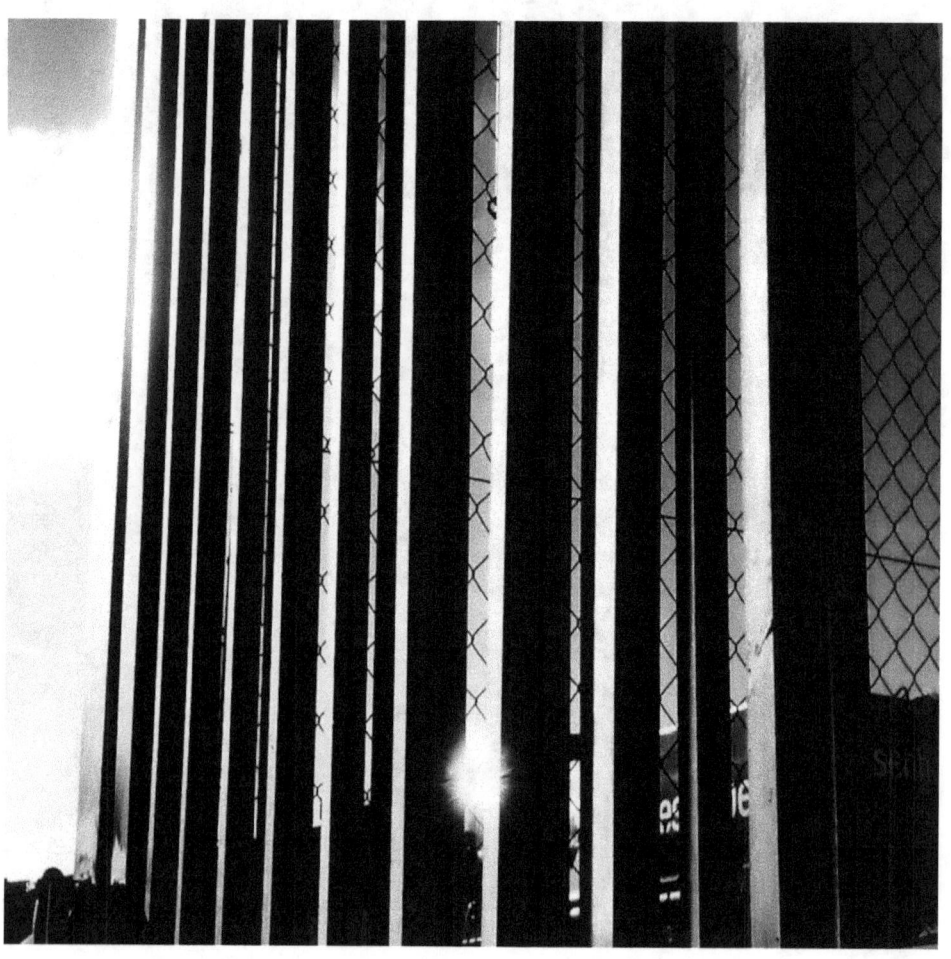

Simone Kaplan			Black & White: Abstract

Simone Kaplan — Black & White: Abstract

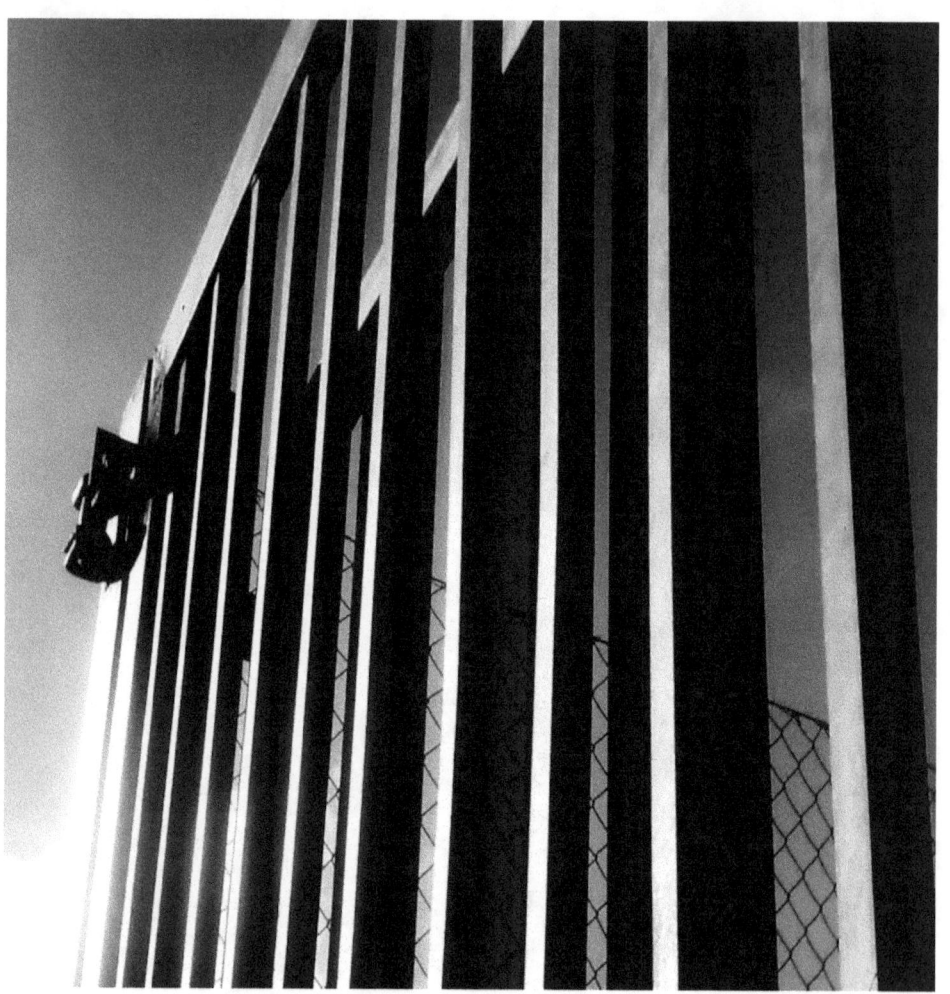

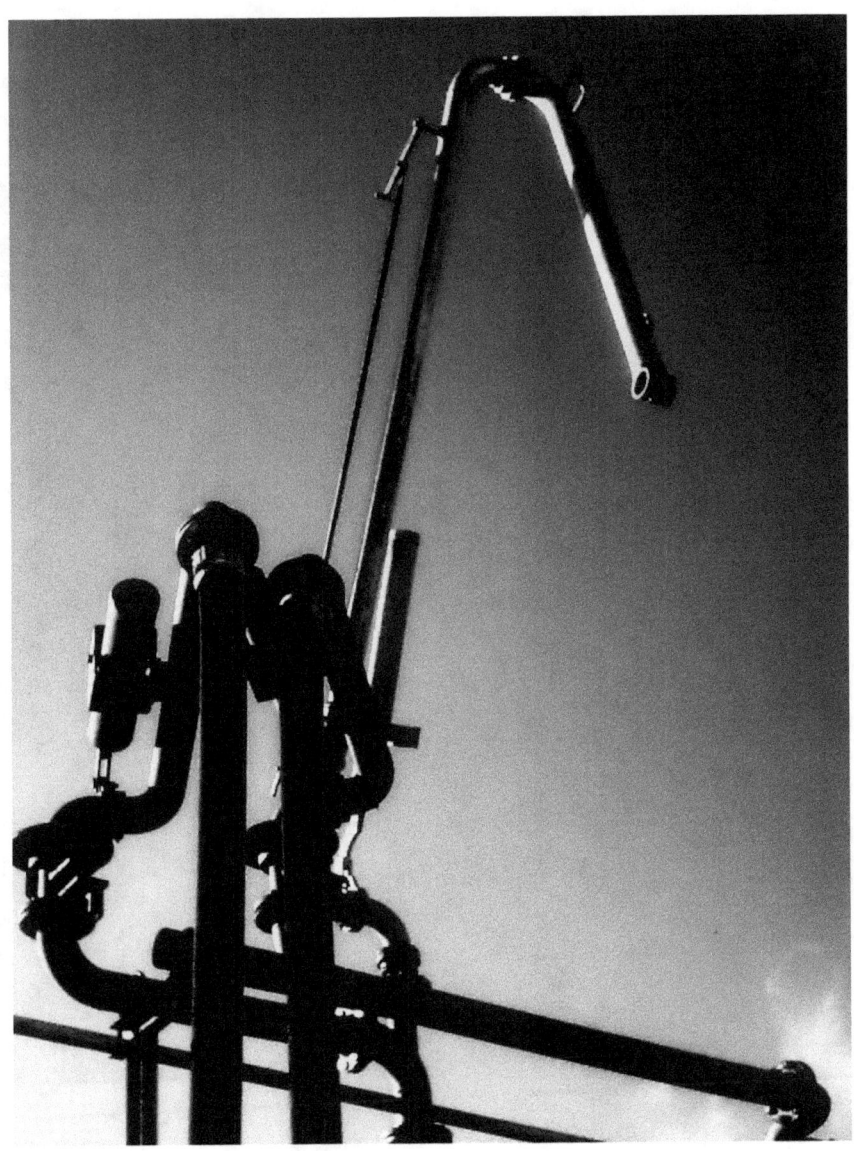

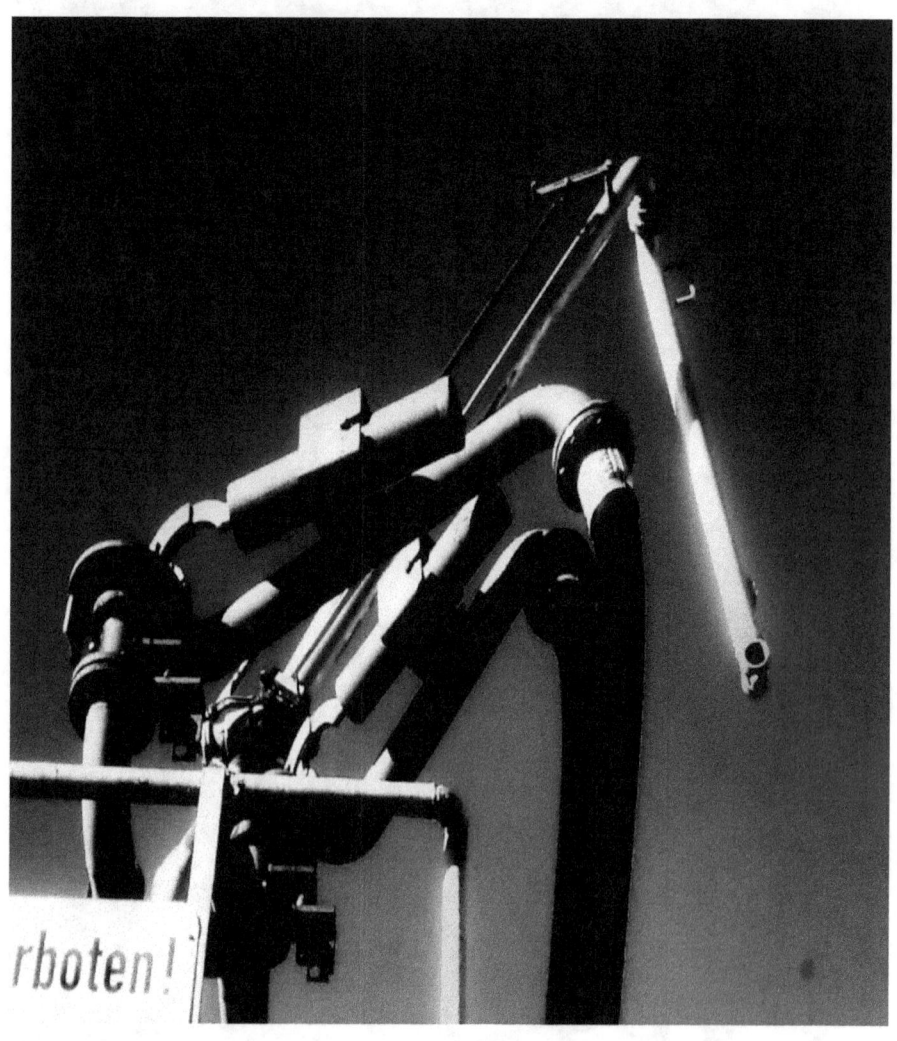

Simone Kaplan   Black & White: Abstract

The Factory Site

The factory site was empty on Sunday. During the week the people worked there. Therefore I chose Sunday to be alone. I still had enough of the last meeting with people.
The tenant with the old filling station hunted to me quite a lot a fright.Here on the factory site no human soul was to be seen far and wide.
I had sunk thus into my world and quite crazily on the different forms and lines .
As the shades longer became I looked up and noted that the sun already set. However, I still wanted to catch the last sunrays also and did not look after my surroundings.

Tired, but contently after a long day, I wanted to leave the factory site when suddenly a sharp voice sounded.
„Stop. Police!!"
I solidified before fright and thought I do not hear properly. Police???
What the hell did the police making here?
I turned around
„What do you make here on the factory site?„
Silently I indicated only at my camera
Immediately my camera was engrossed as well as my identity card.
A policeman went with it to the car, the other stopped beside me and guarded me strictly.
I only stood there and trembled with cold and fear.
I had no notion what the policemen with myself planned.
After an eternity appeared other again and returned to me the identity card and the camera.
„Nice pictures.„ ‚he smiling.

Finally, they cleared up me that a phone call would have come, a person would hang around on the factory site and already since hours.
They held me for a "burglar".!!!

And well... have a good time with these pictures of the factory site.

Simone Kaplan   Black & White: Abstract

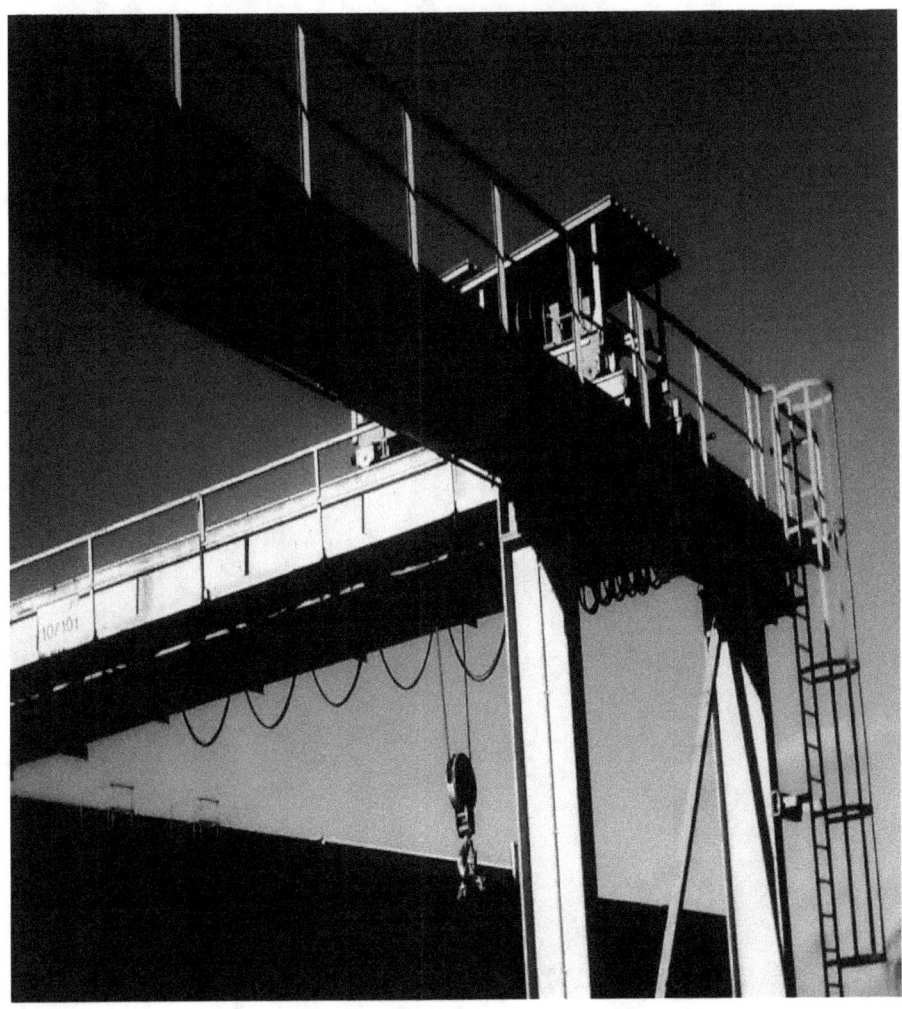

Simone Kaplan — Black & White: Abstract

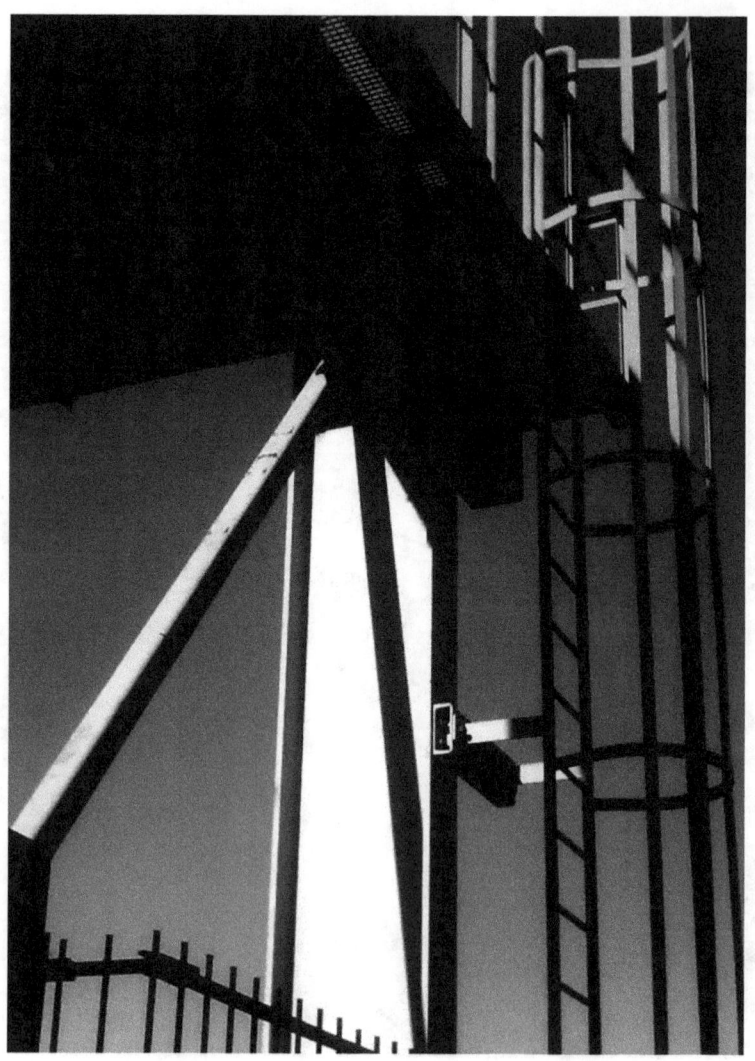

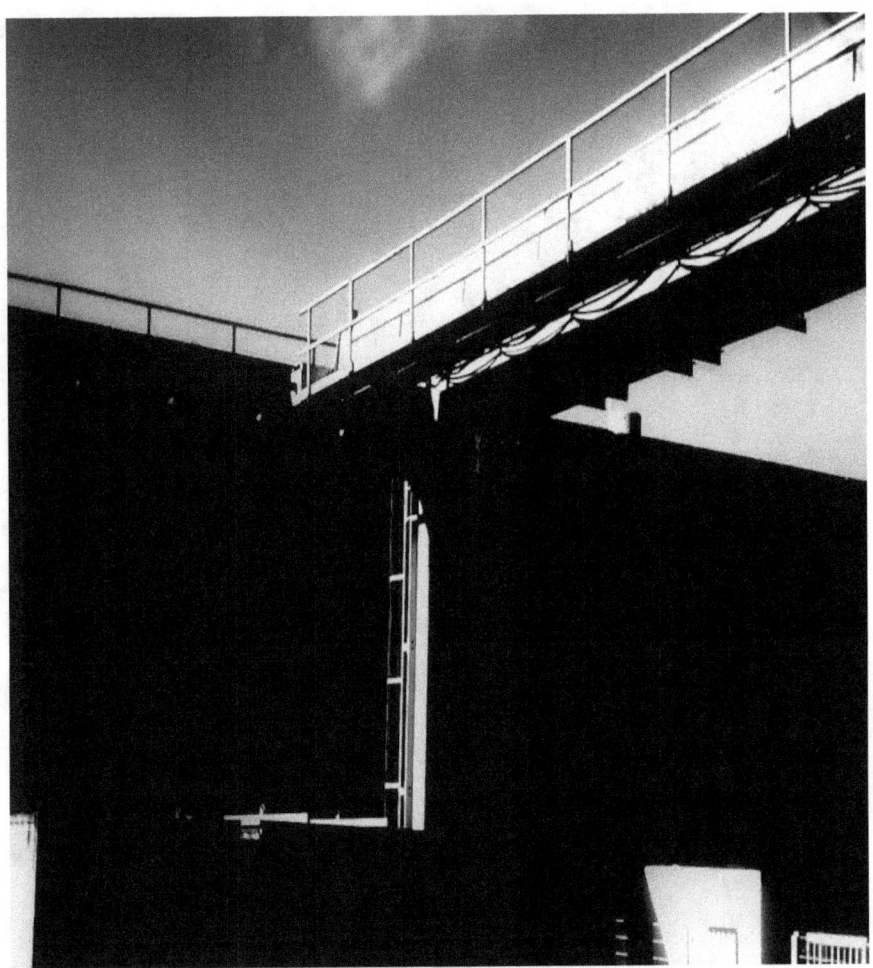

Simone Kaplan   Black & White: Abstract

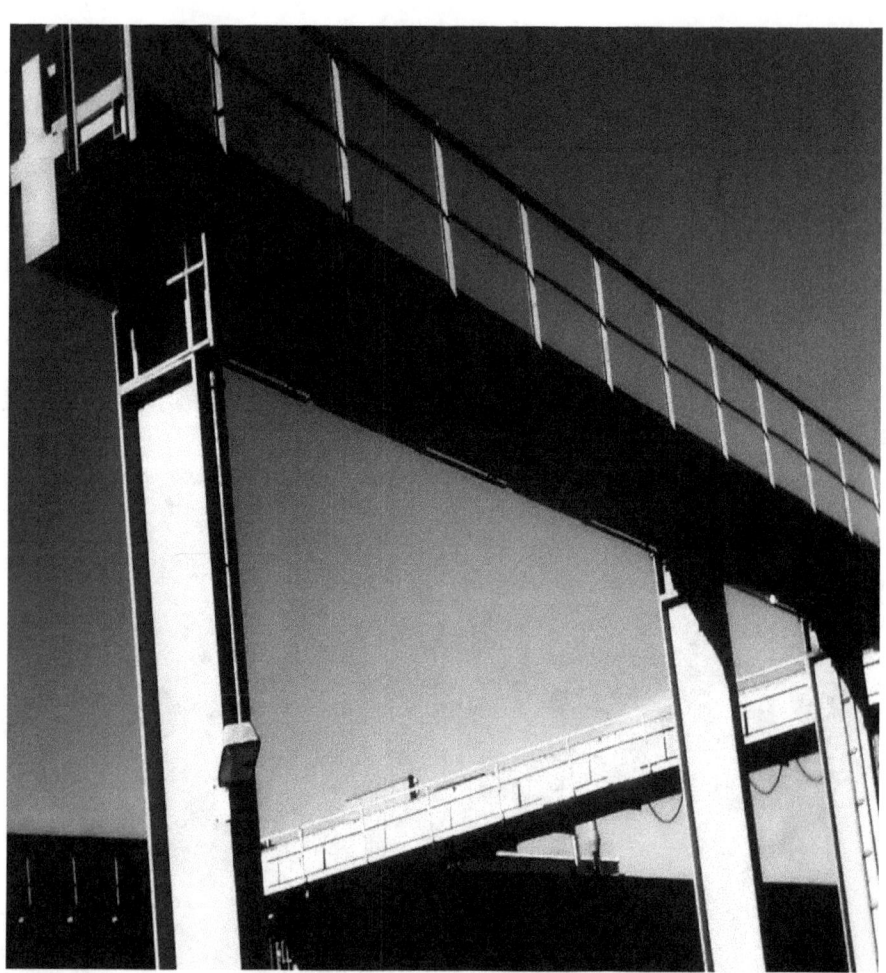

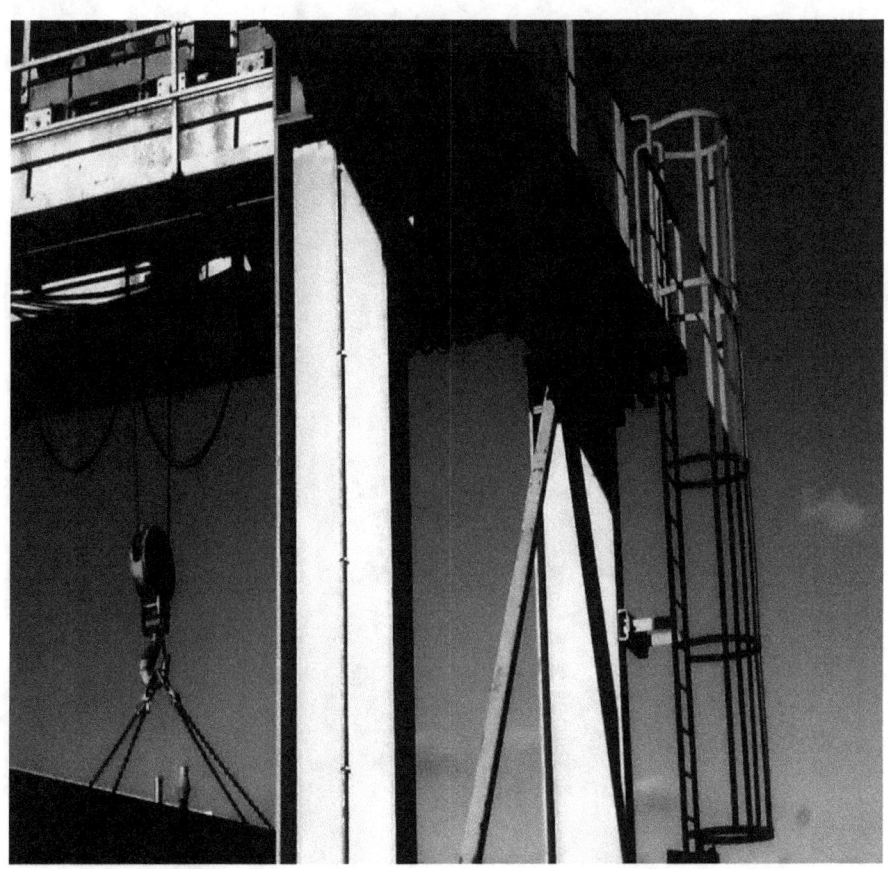

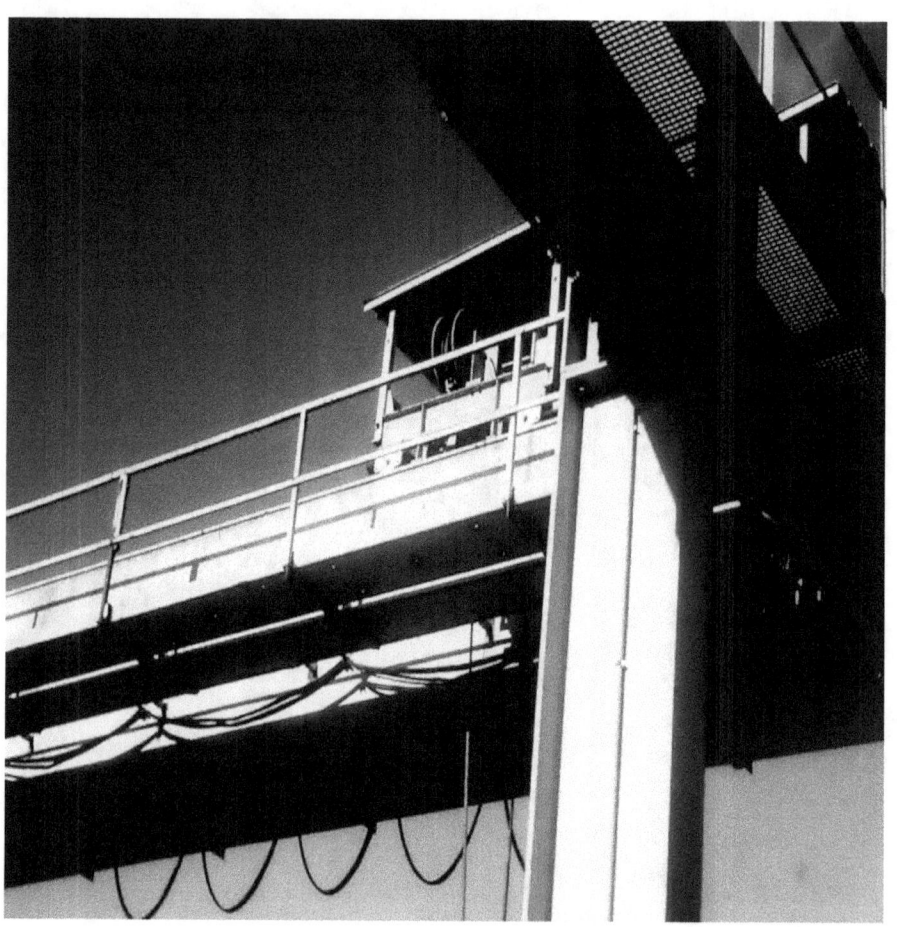

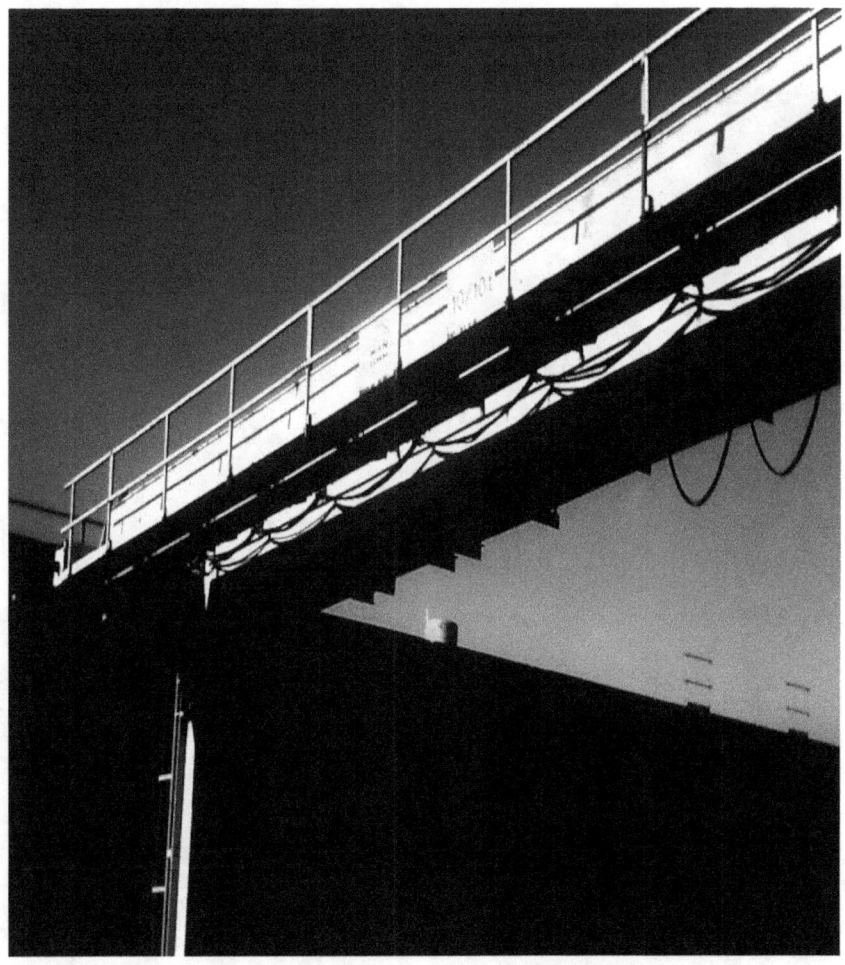

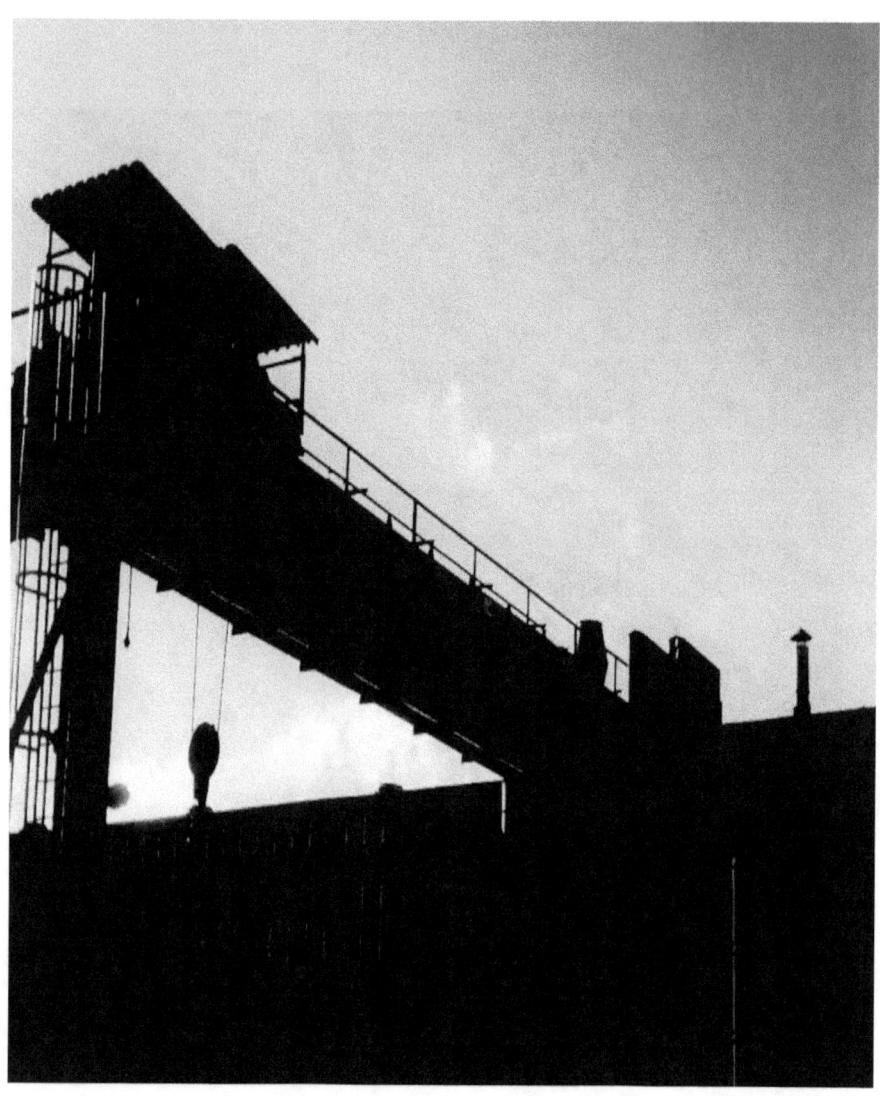

Simone Kaplan — Black & White: Abstract

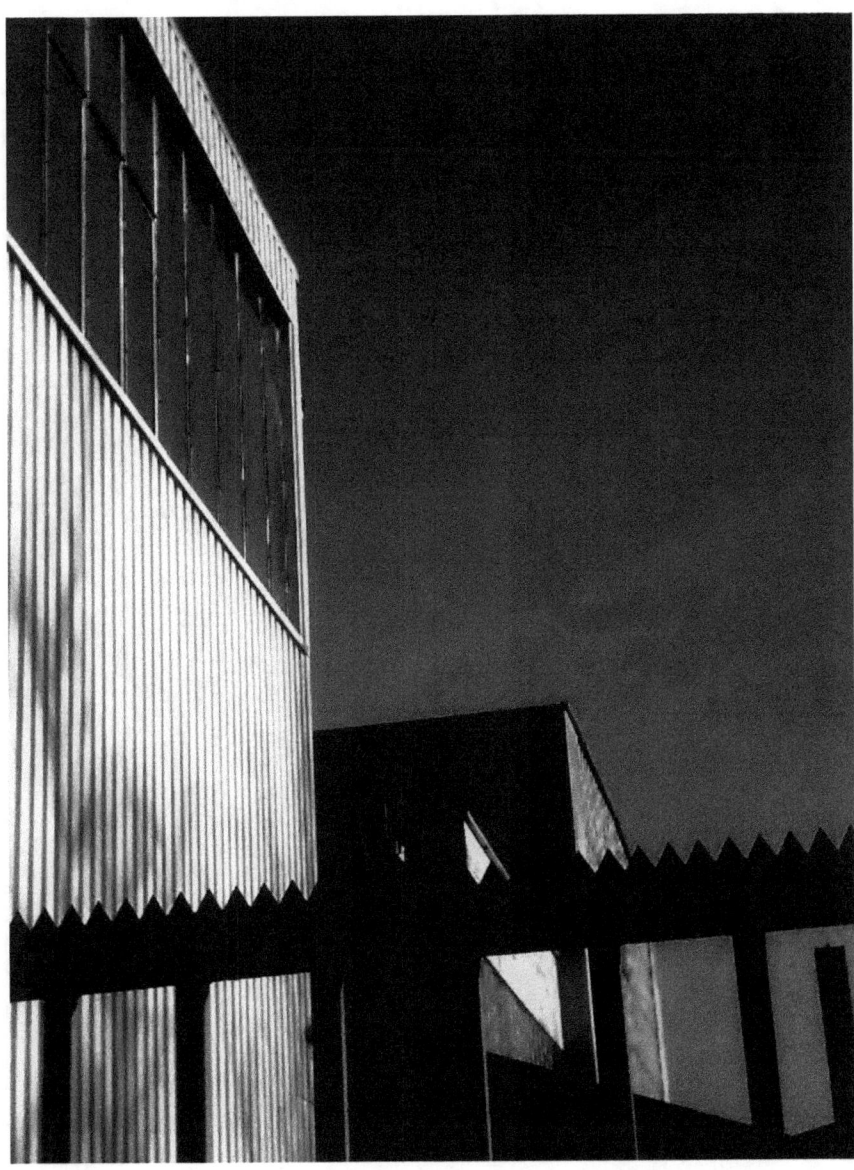

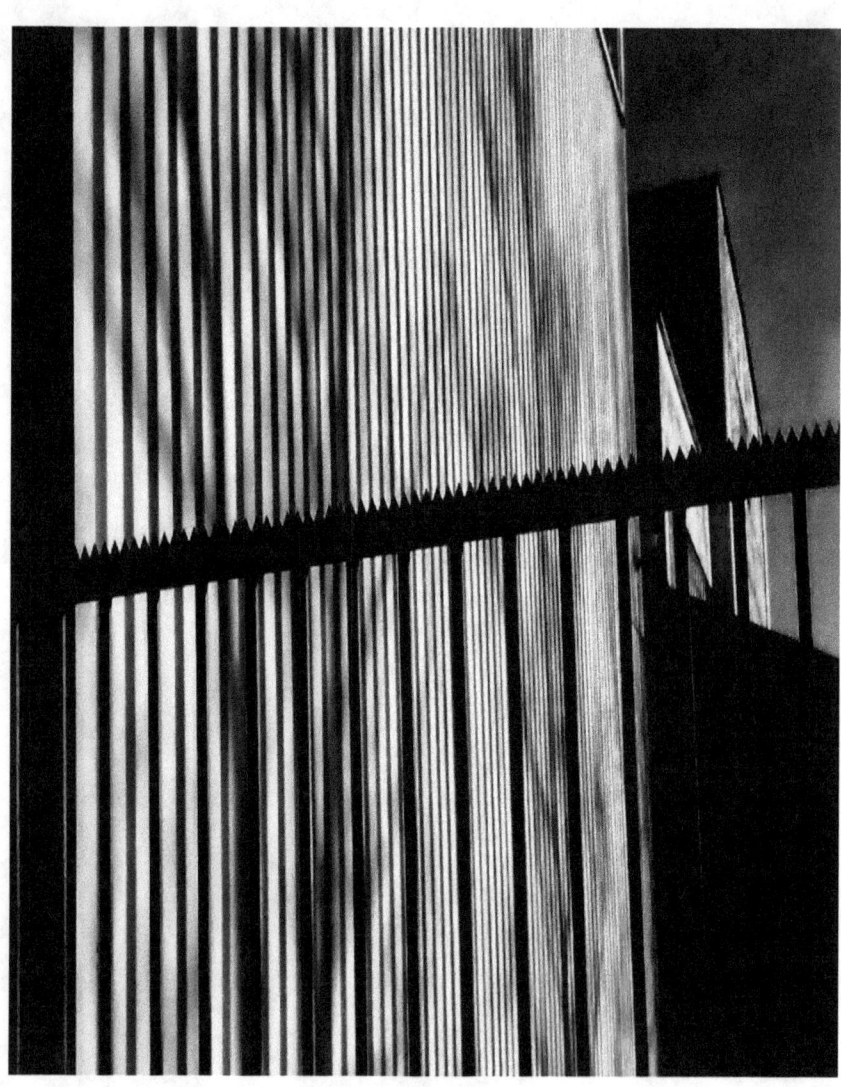

Simone Kaplan Black & White: Abstract

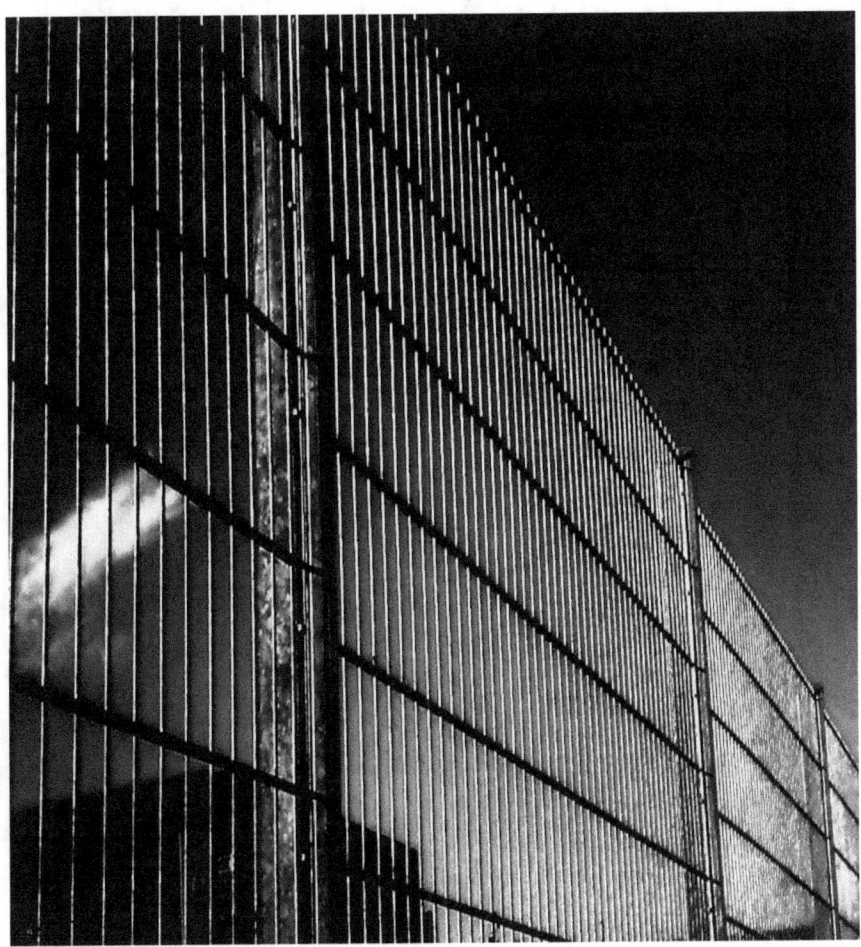

Simone Kaplan   Black & White: Abstract

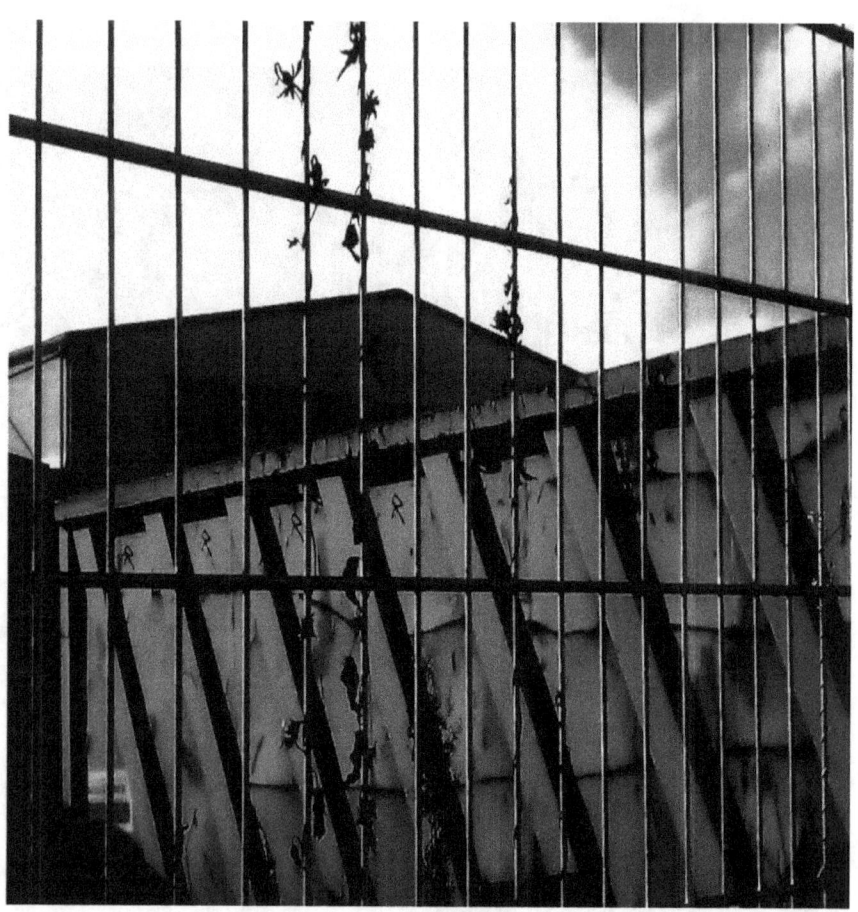

Simone Kaplan Black & White: Abstract

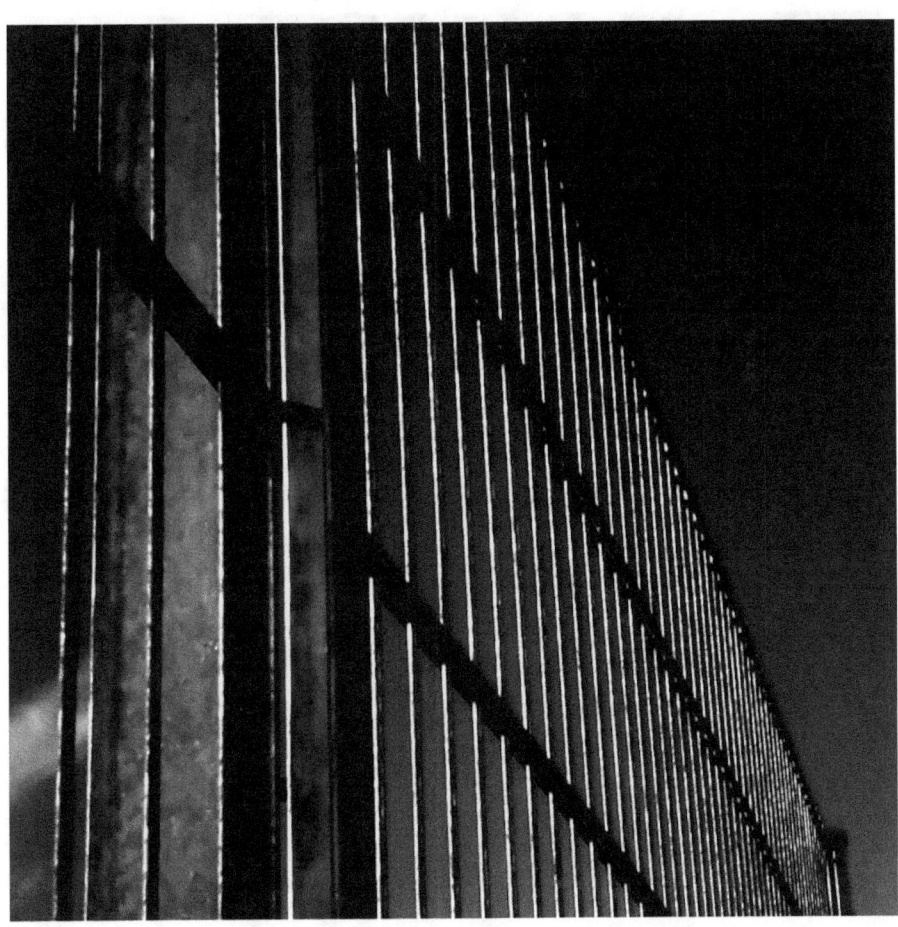

Simone Kaplan   Black & White: Abstract

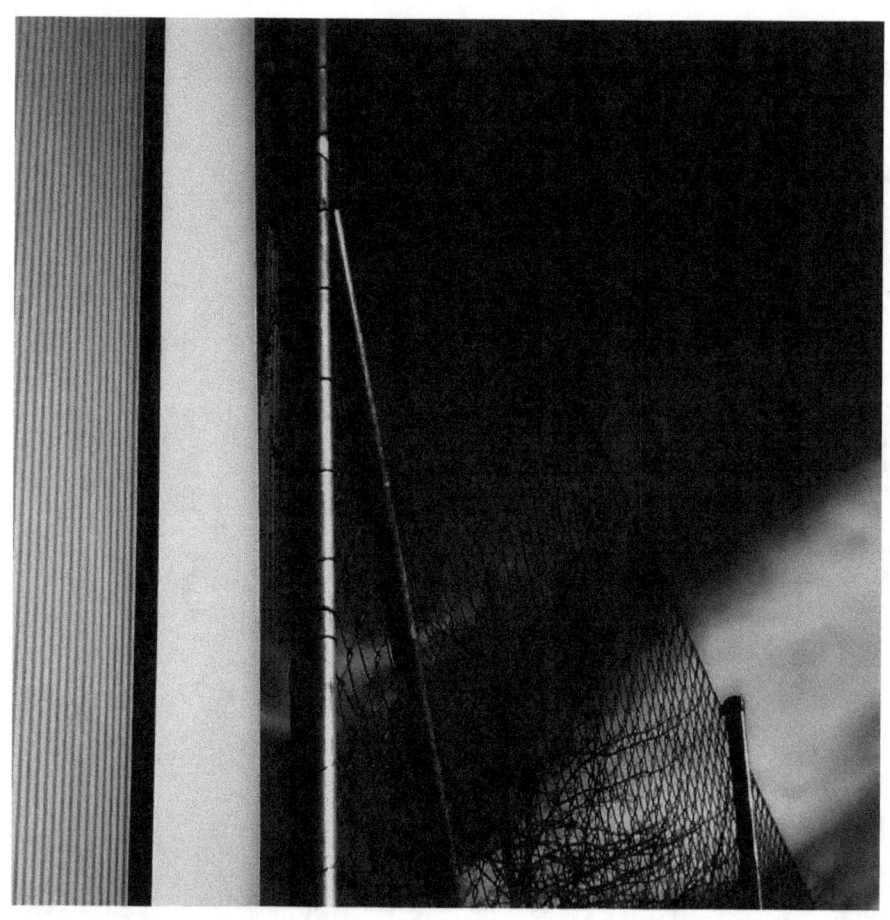

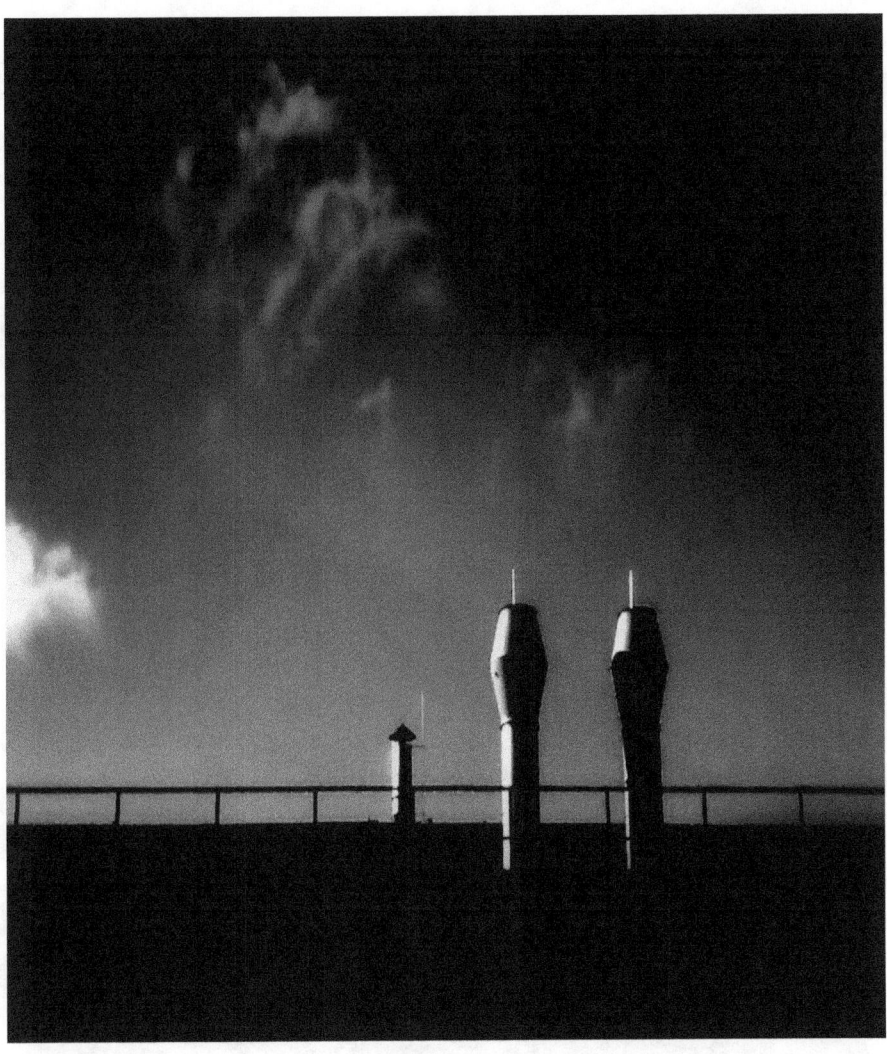

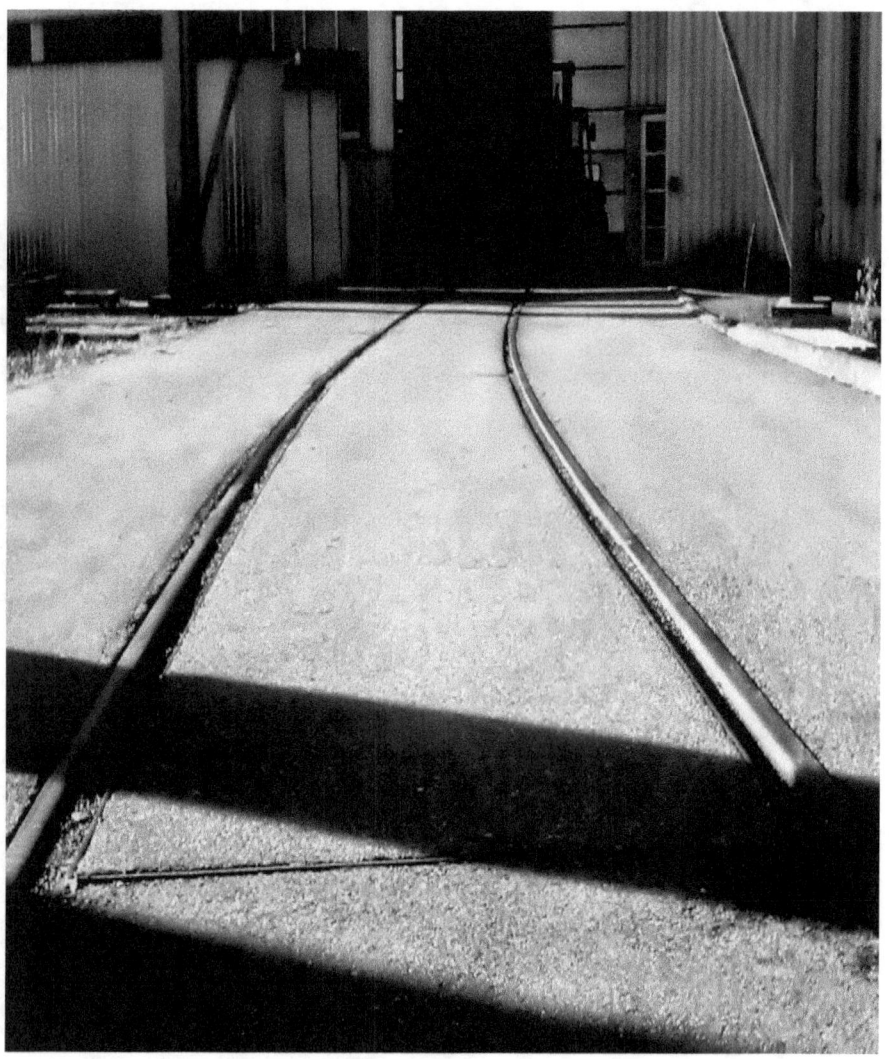

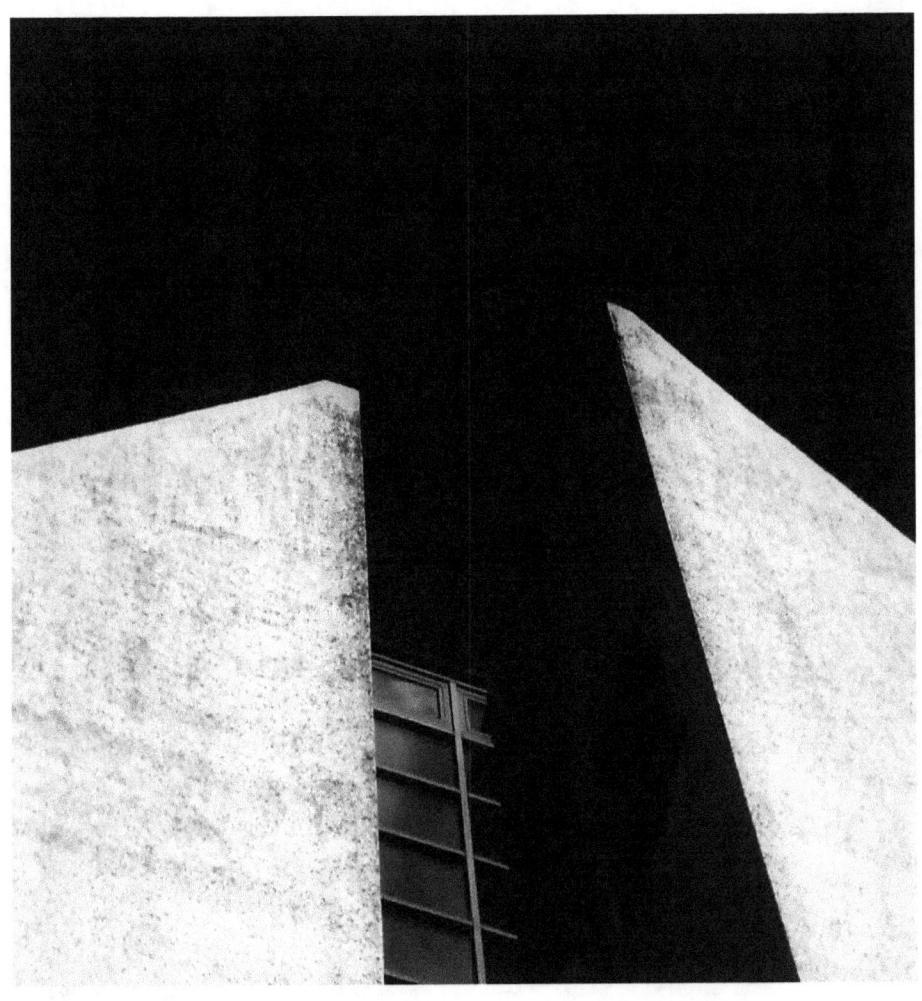

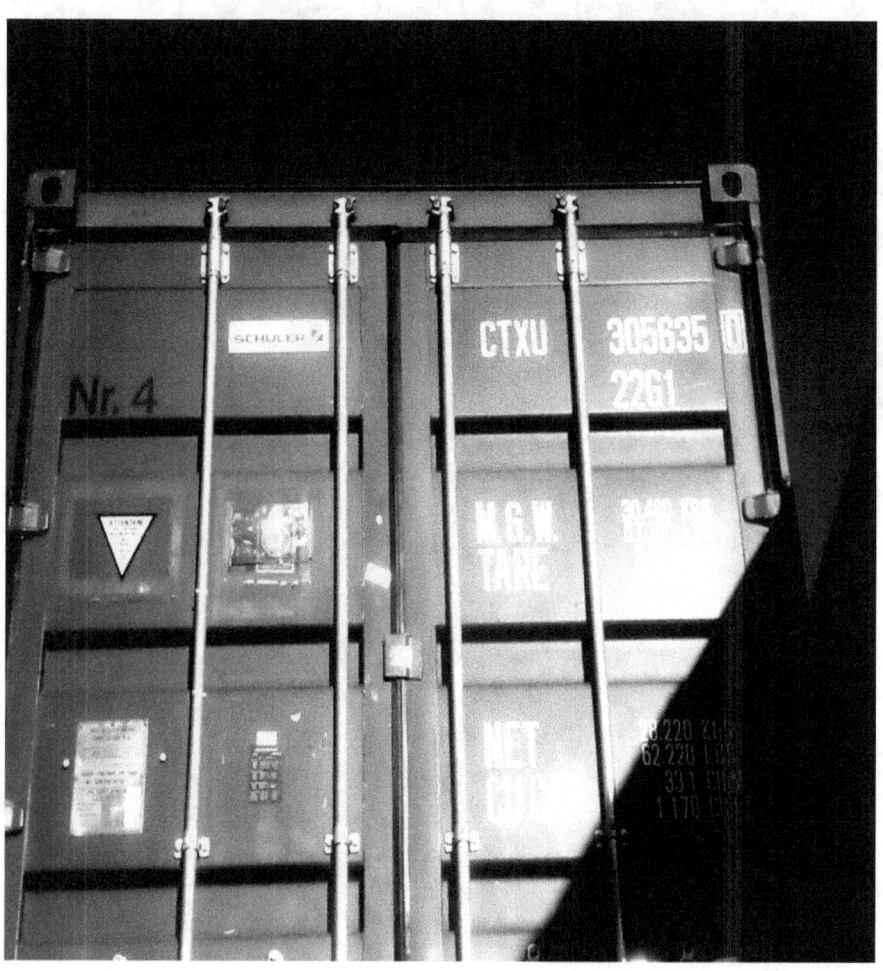

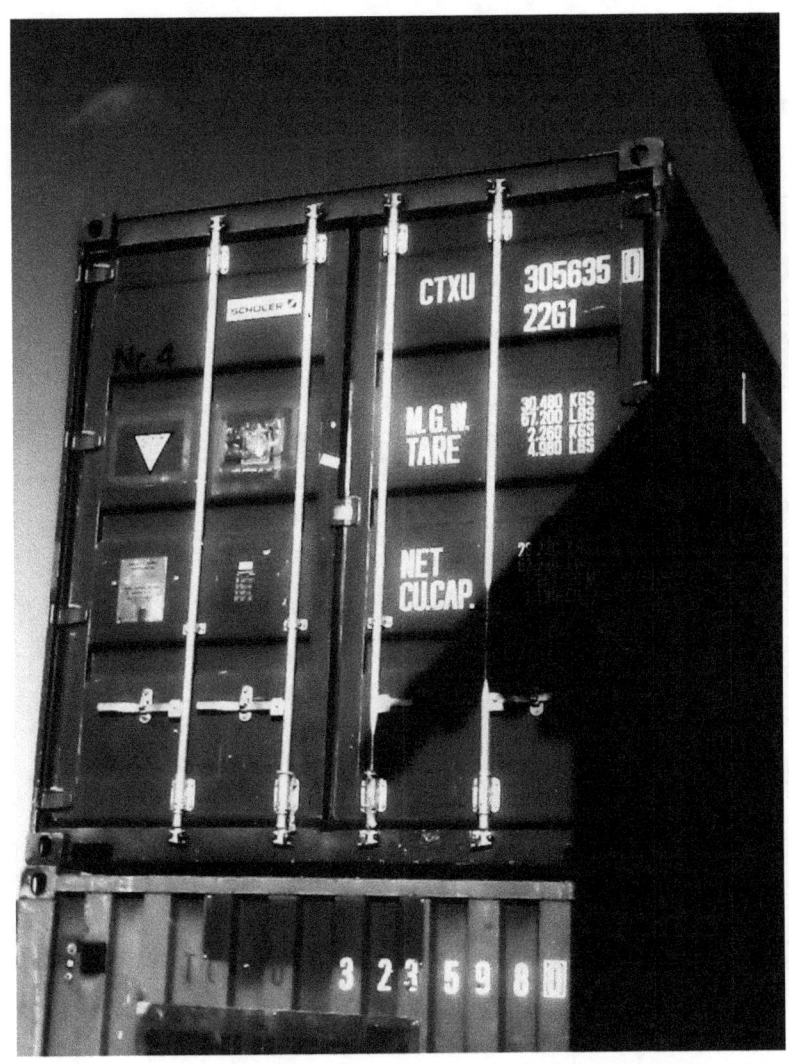

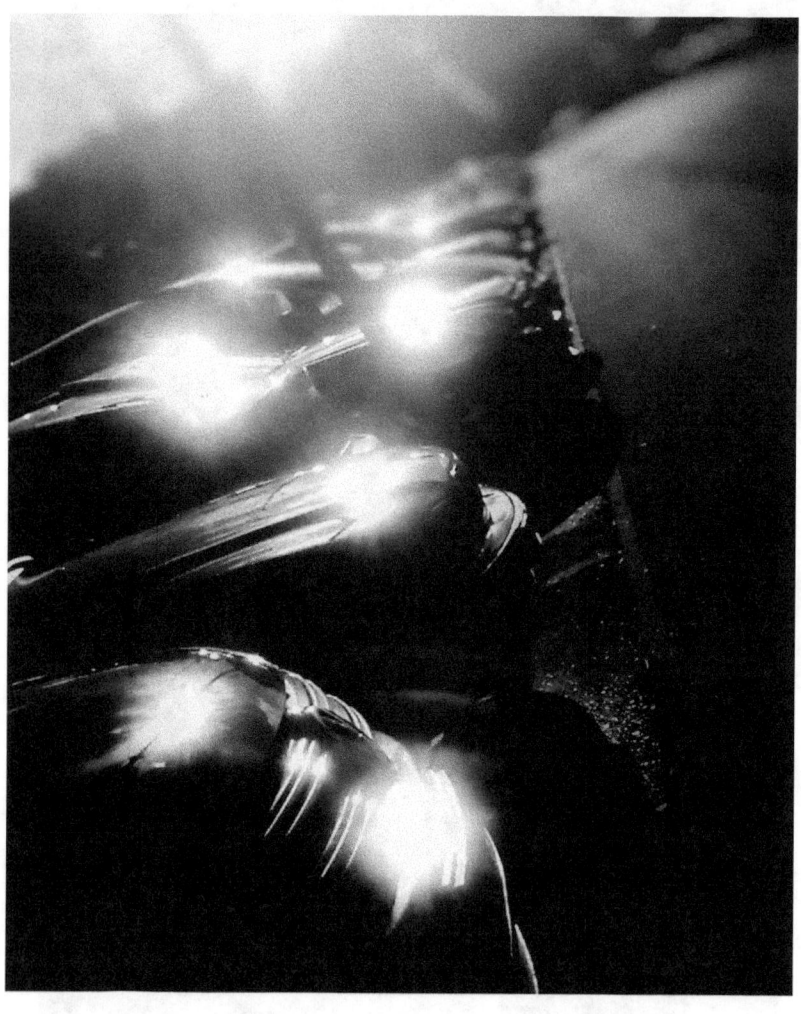

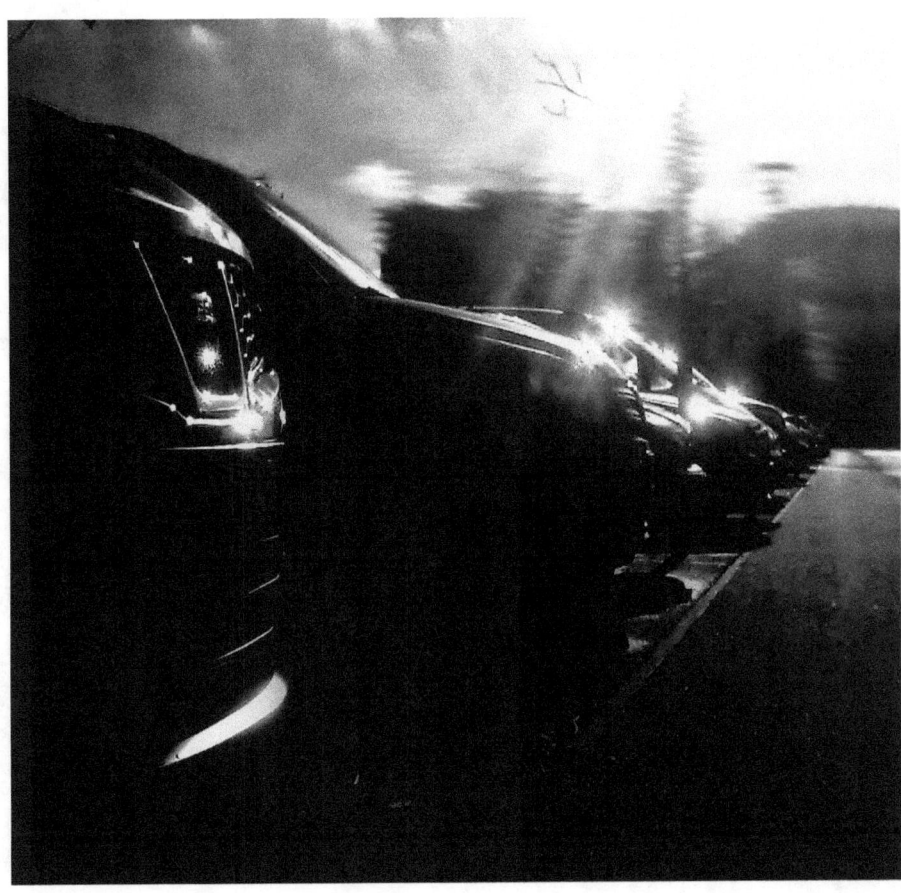

Simone Kaplan Black & White: Abstract

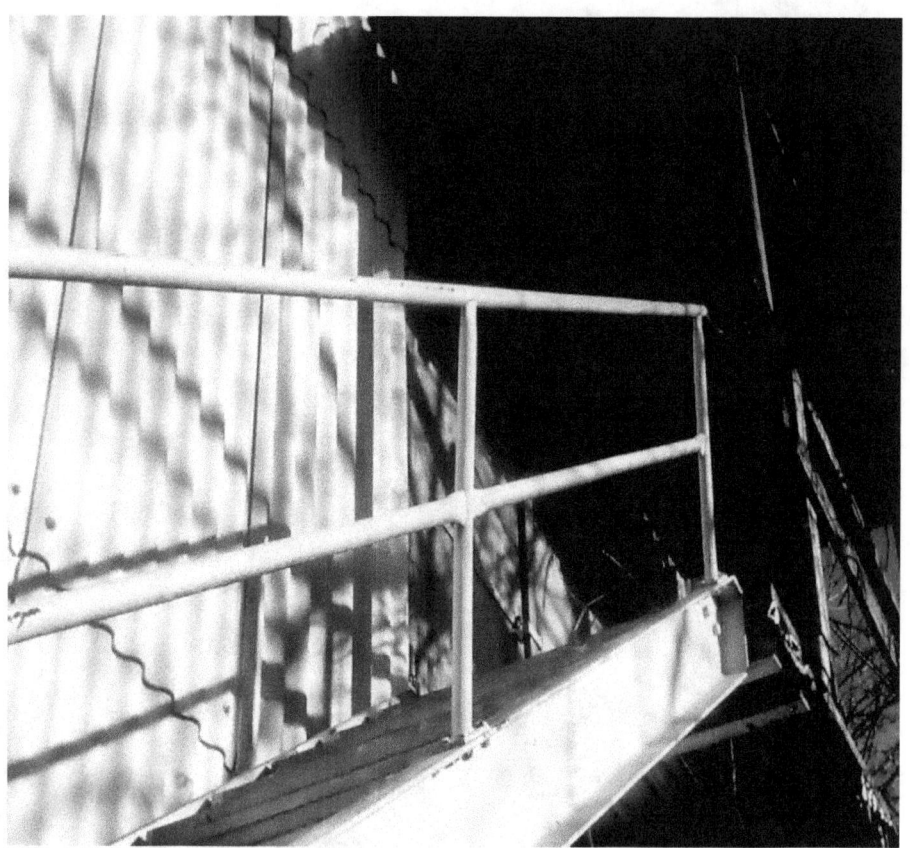

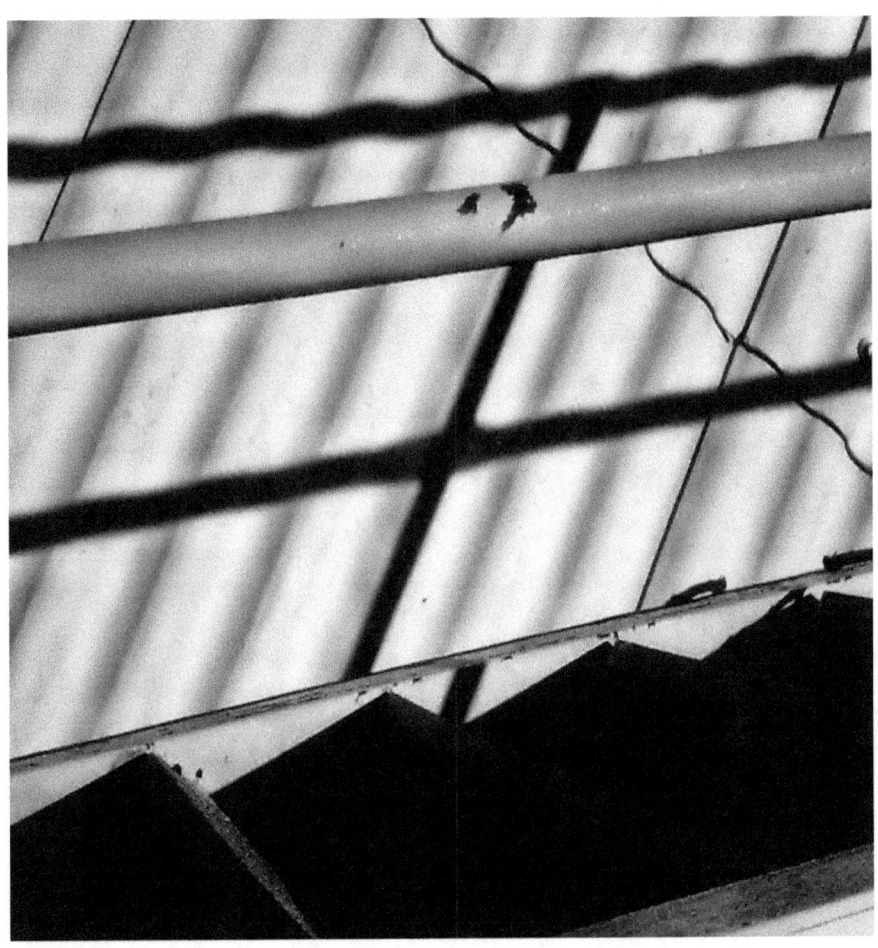

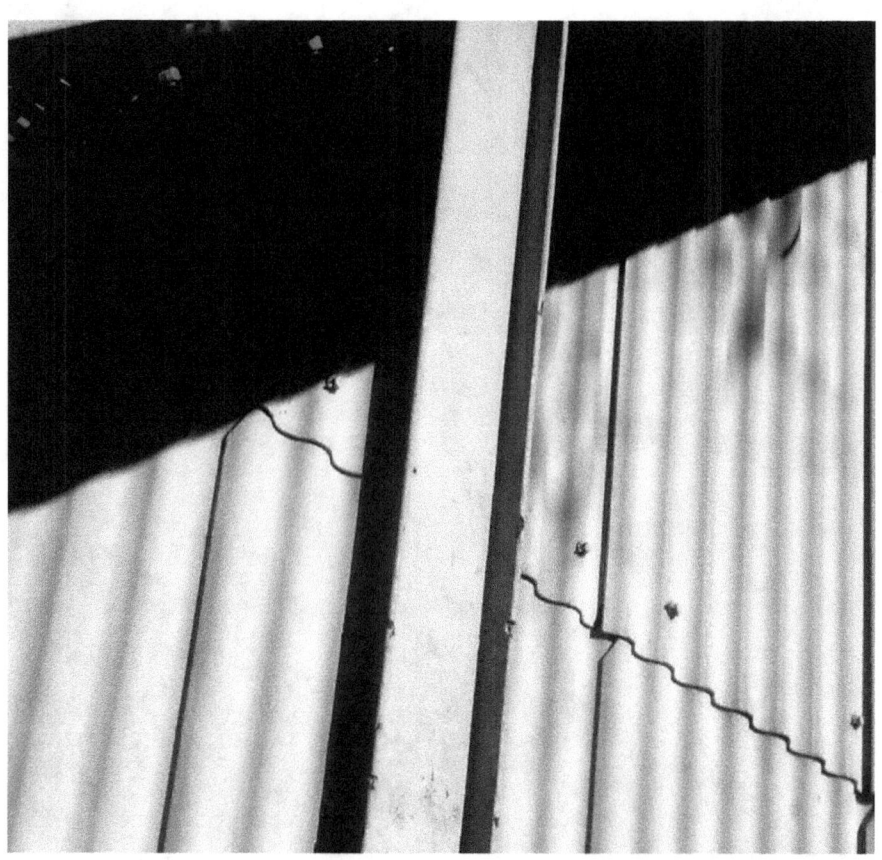

Simone Kaplan   Black & White: Abstract

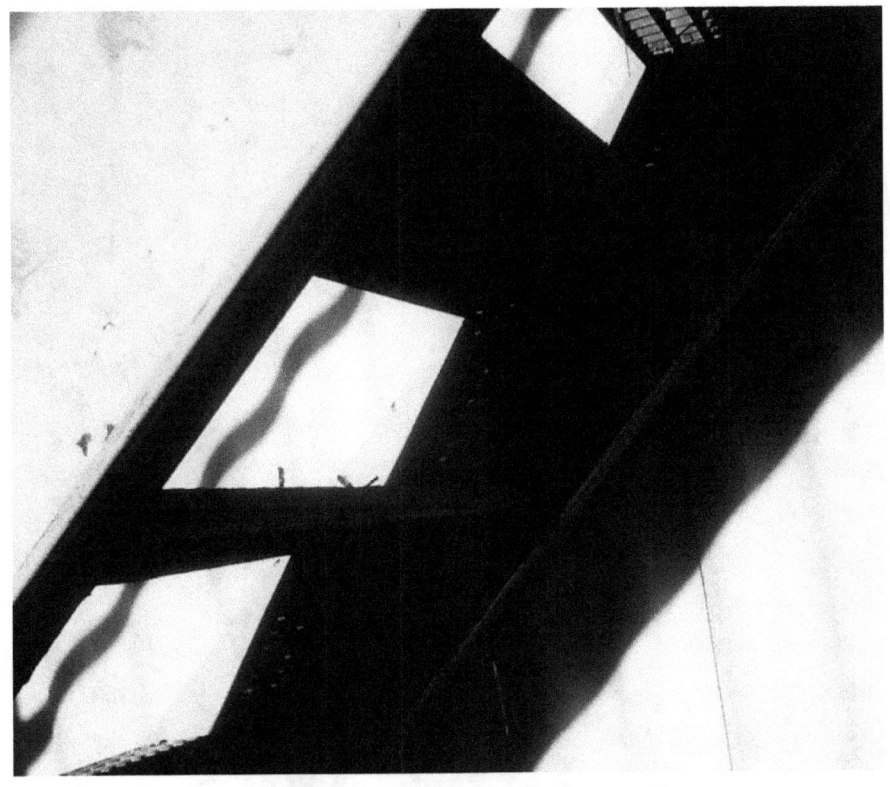

Simone Kaplan — Black & White: Abstract

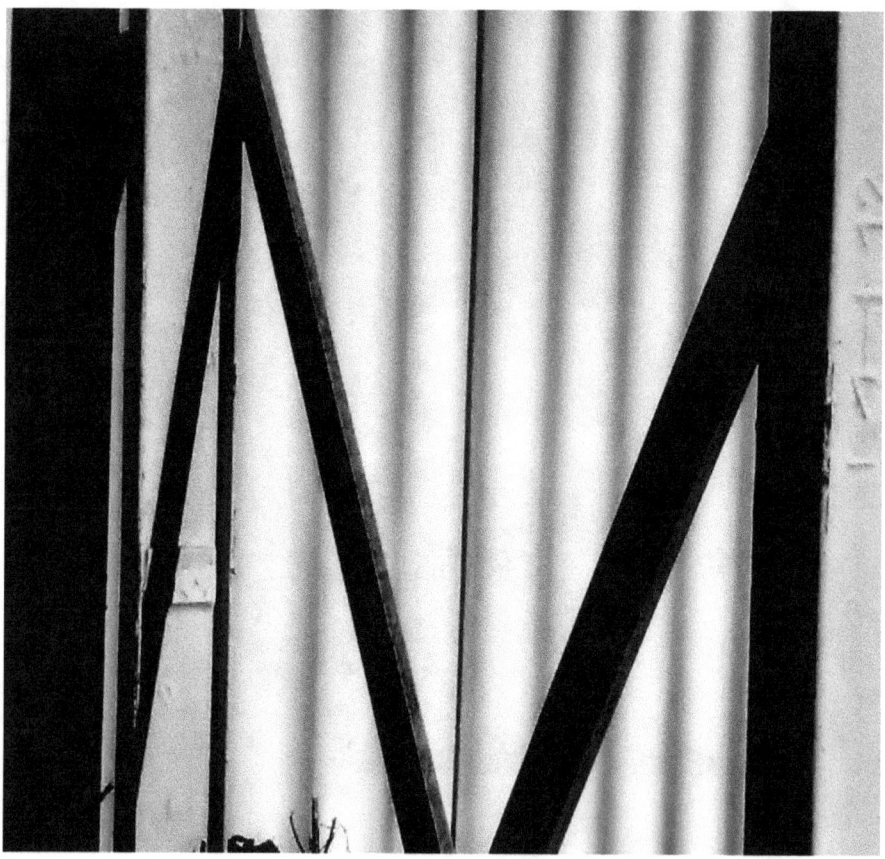

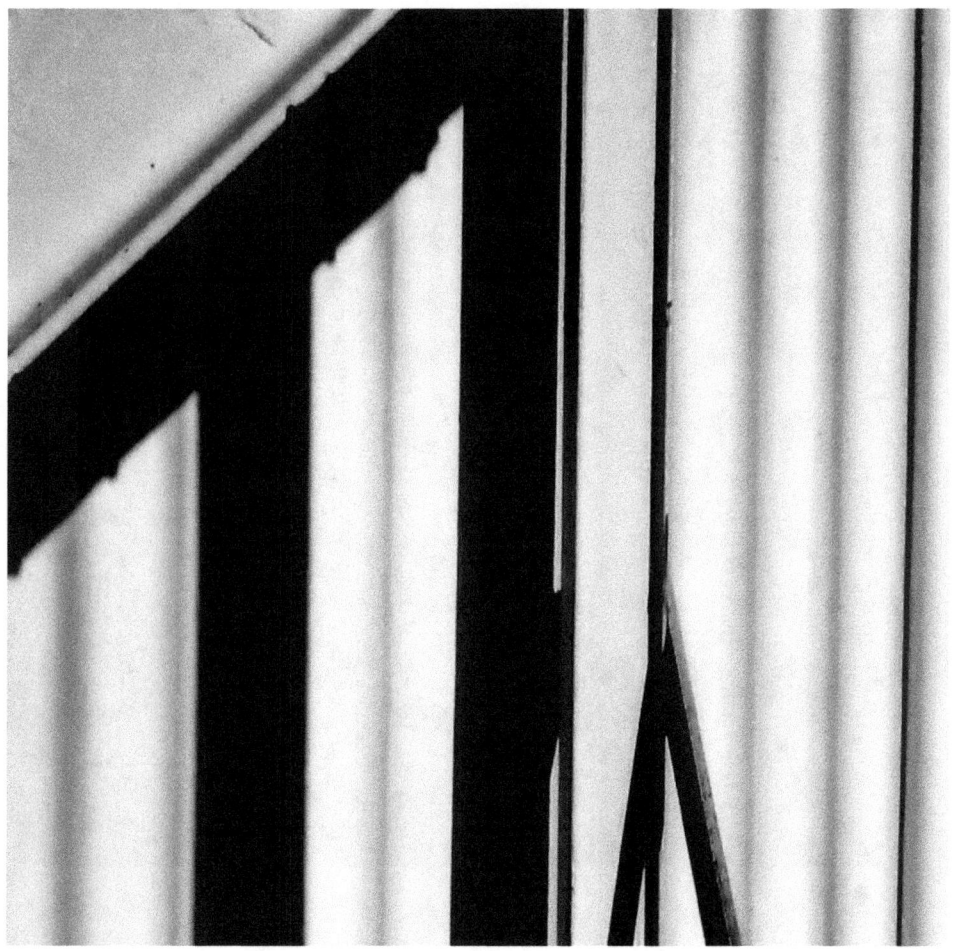

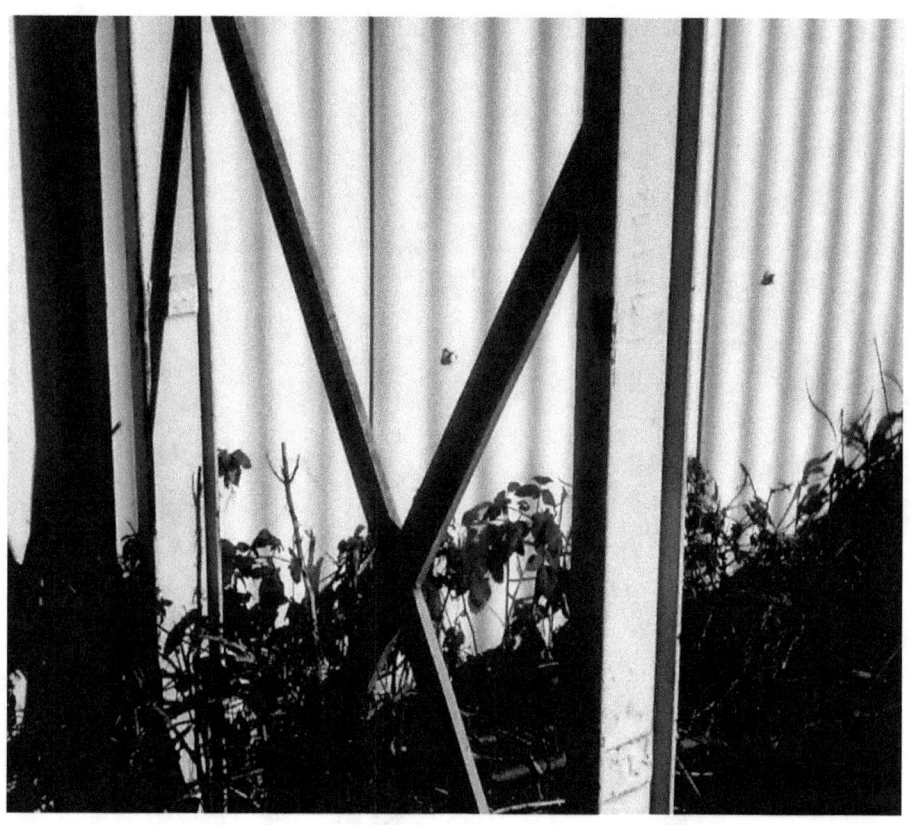

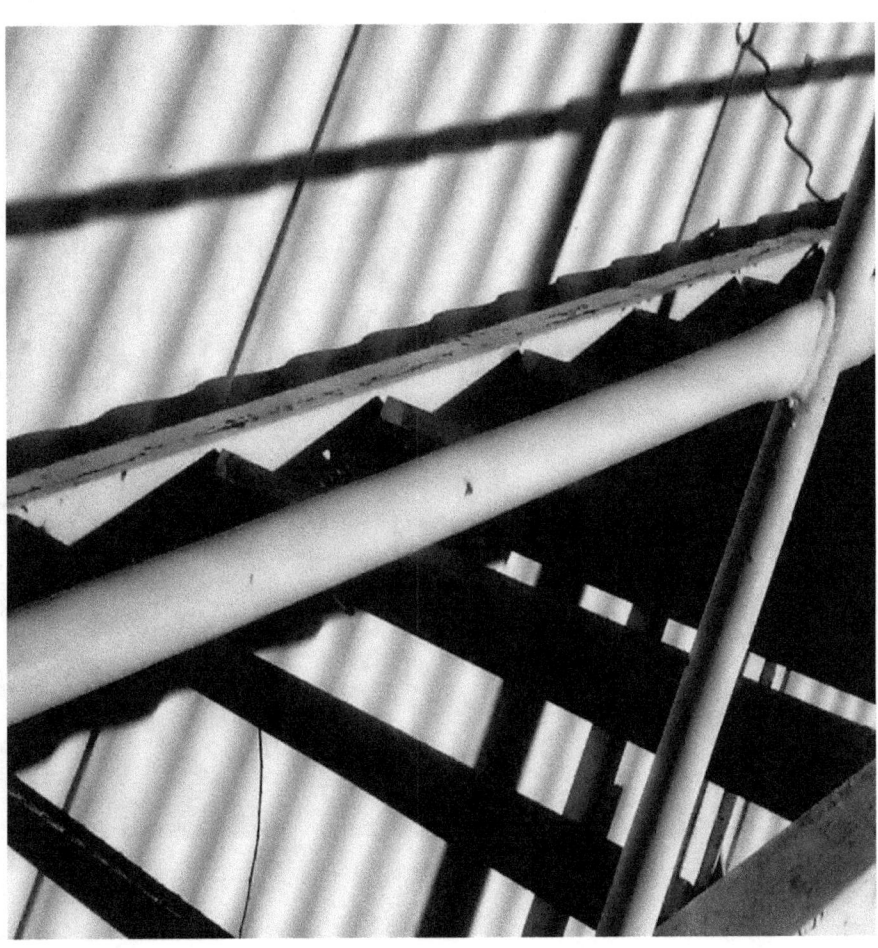

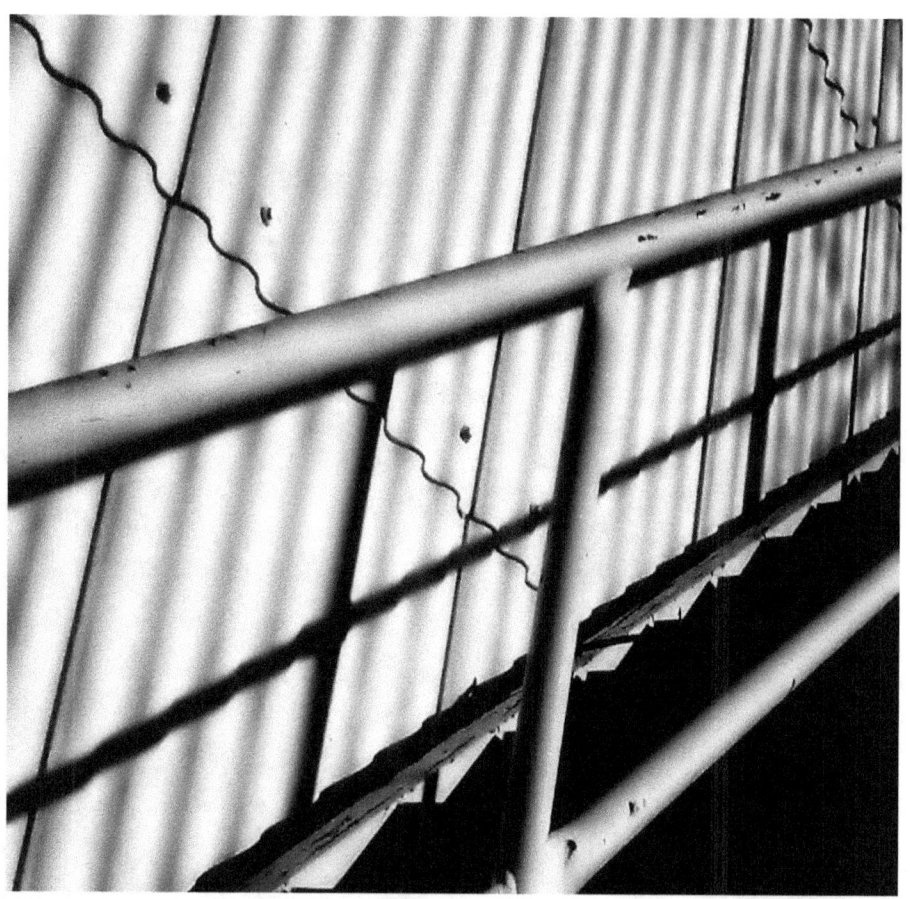

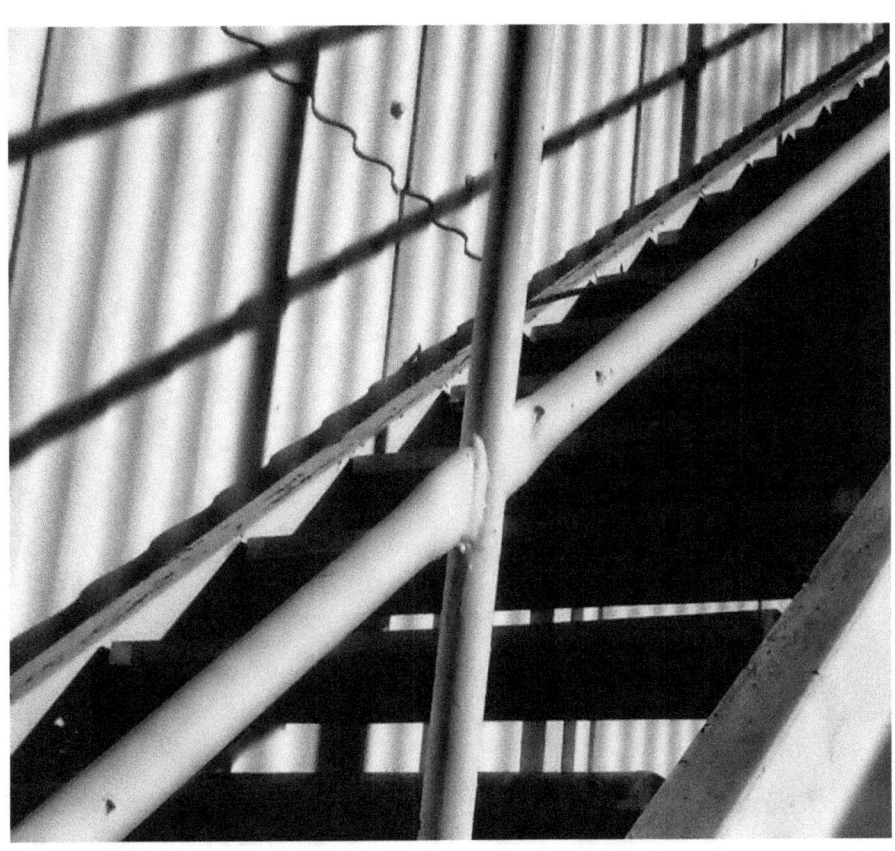

Simone Kaplan	Black & White: Abstract

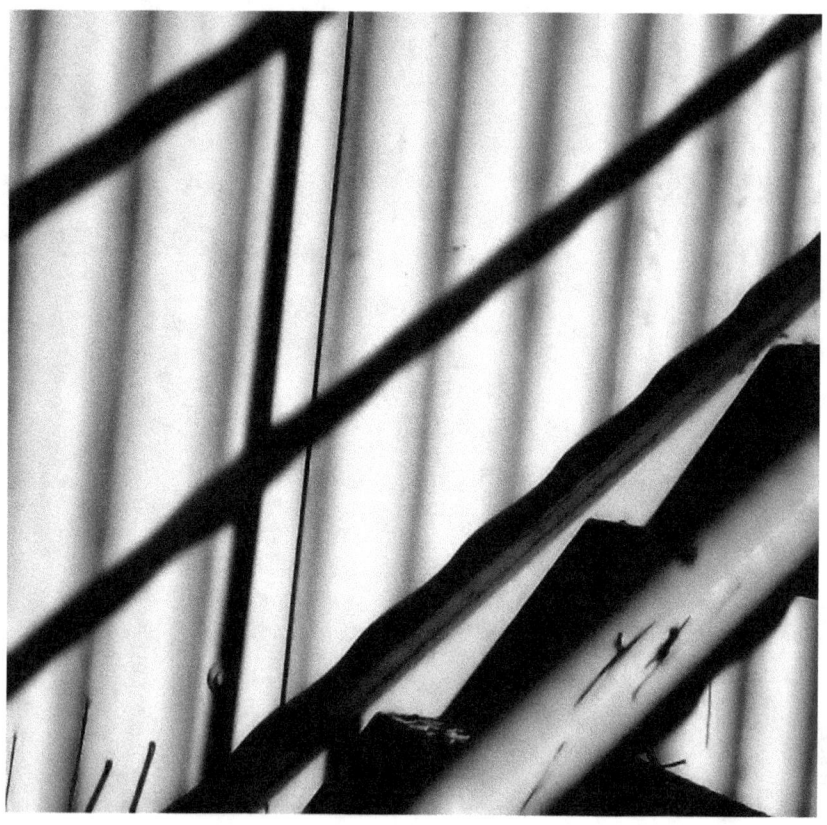

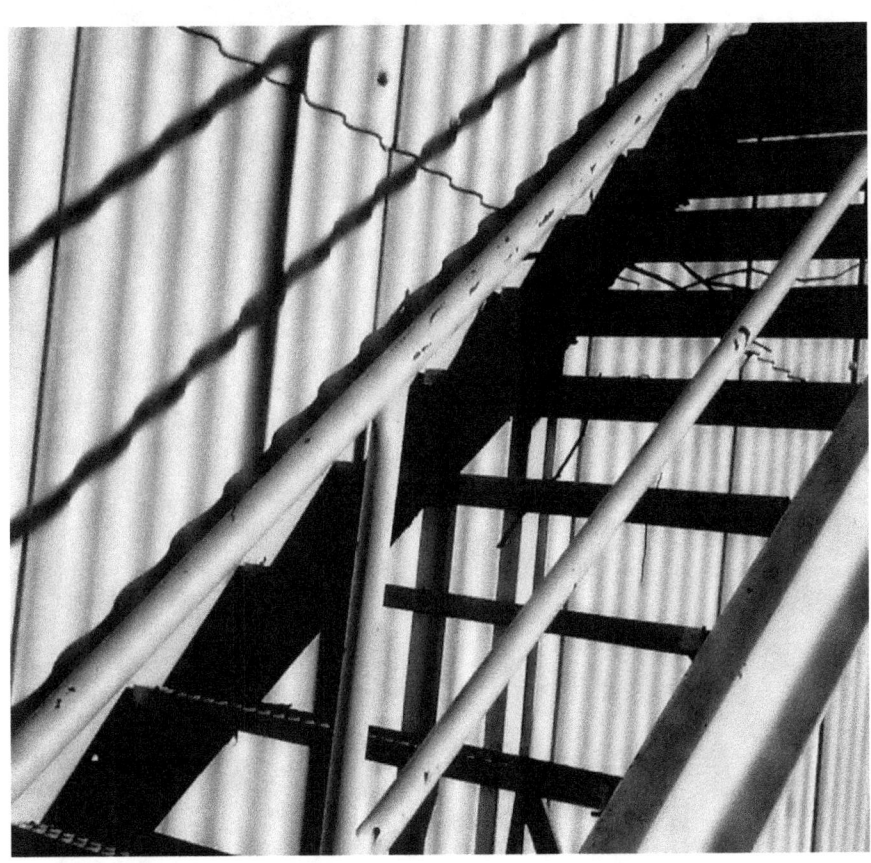

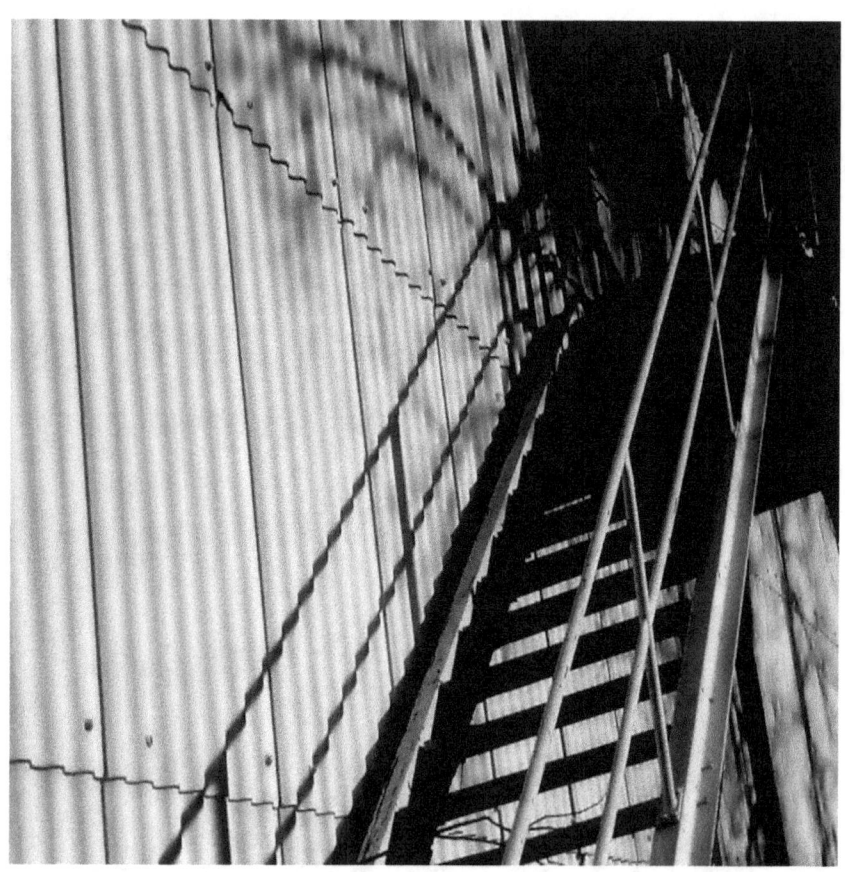

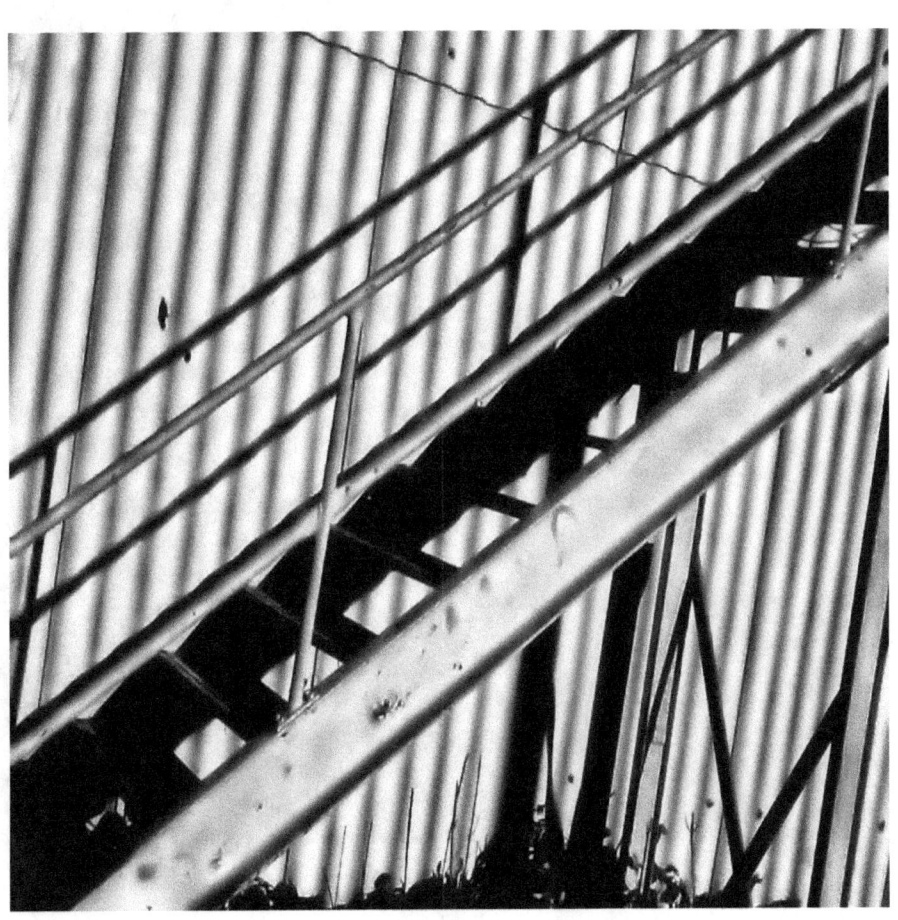

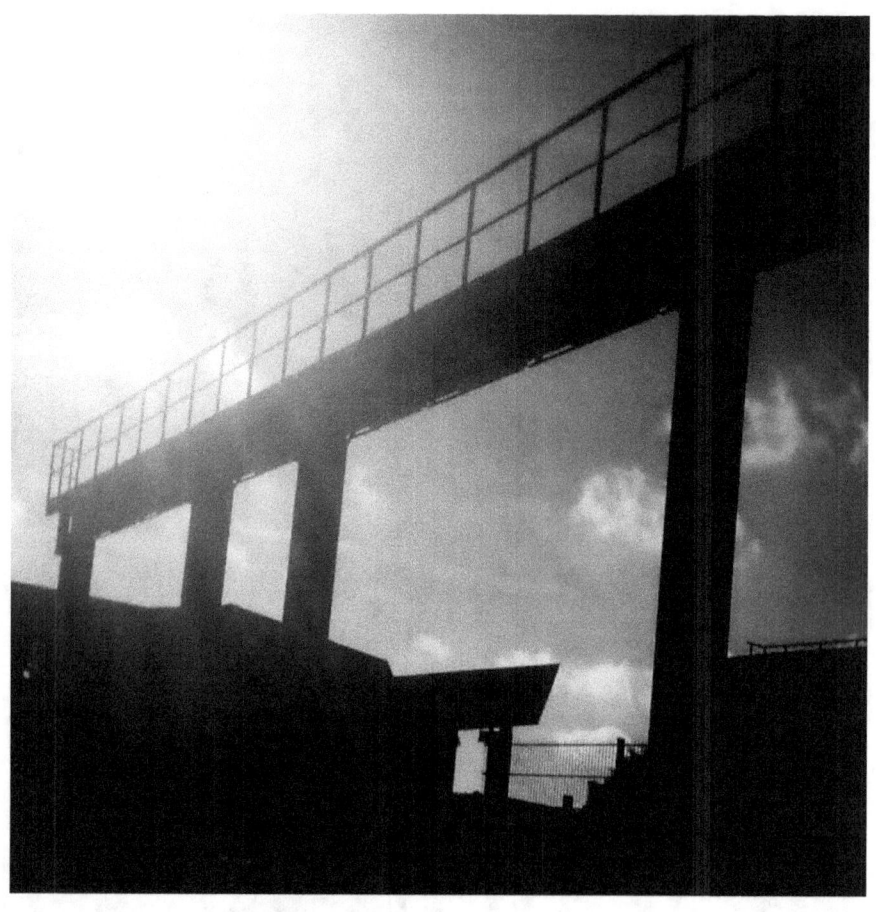

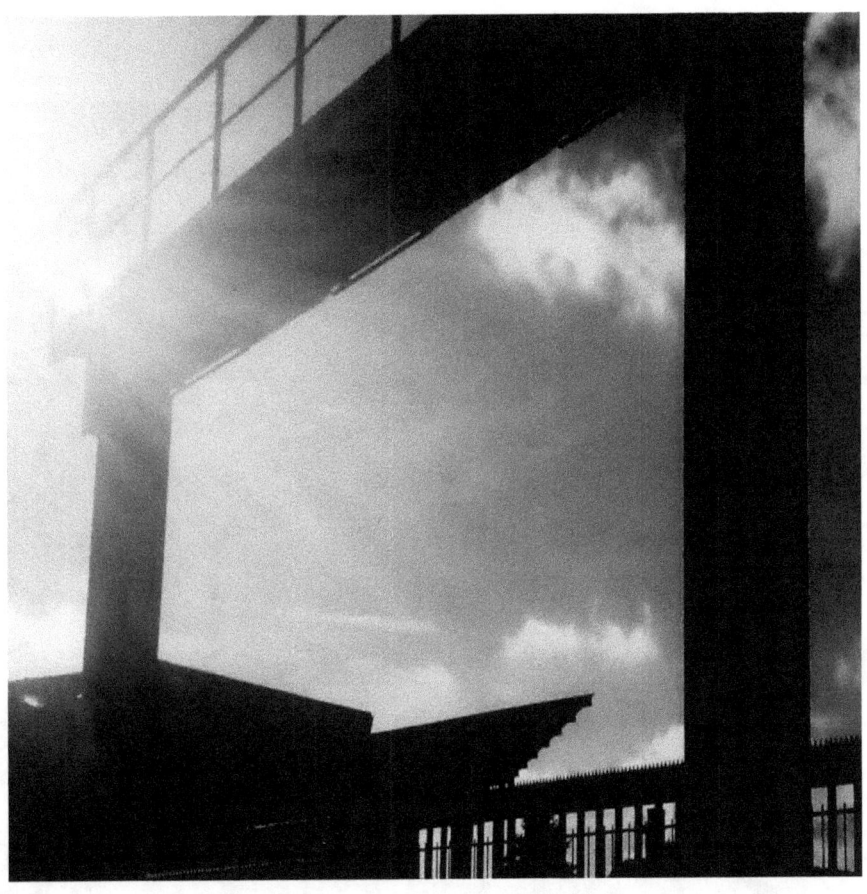

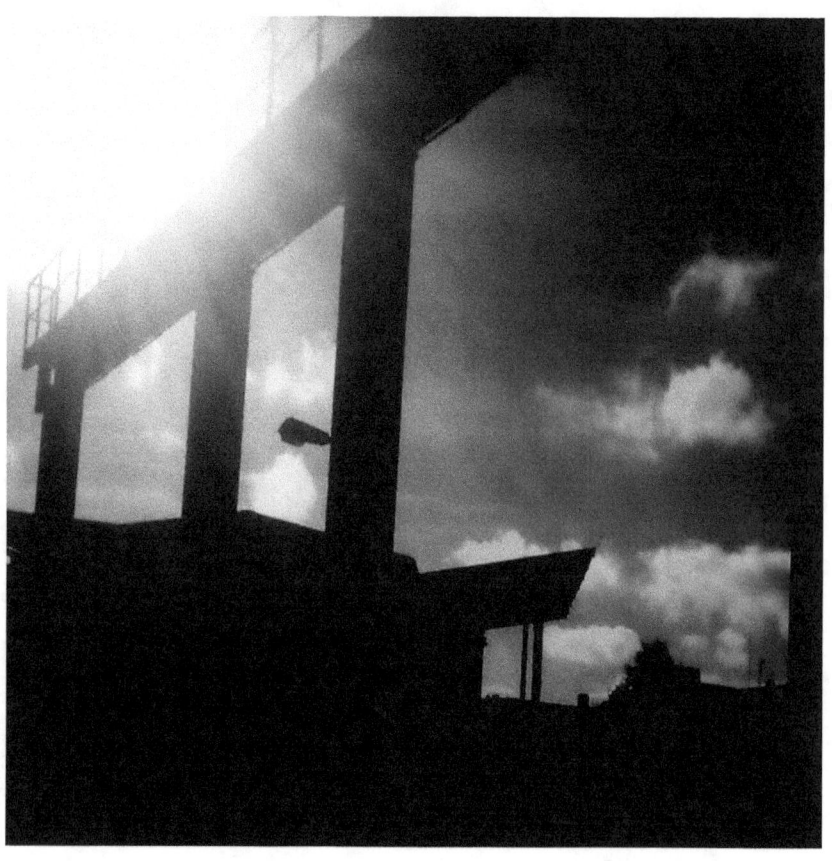

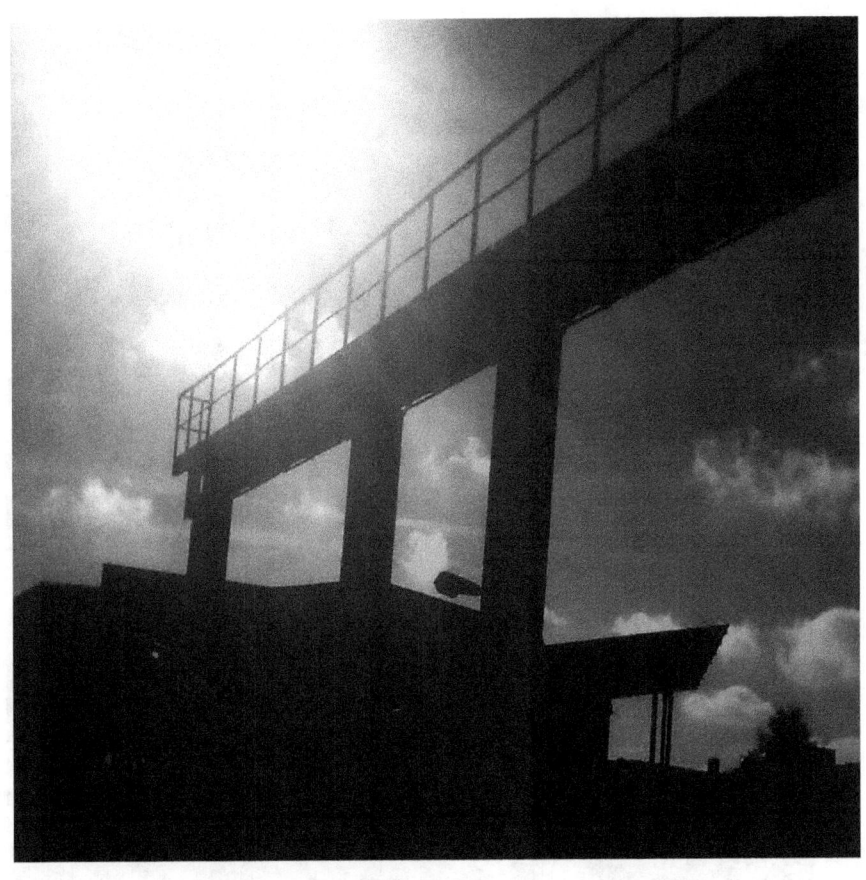

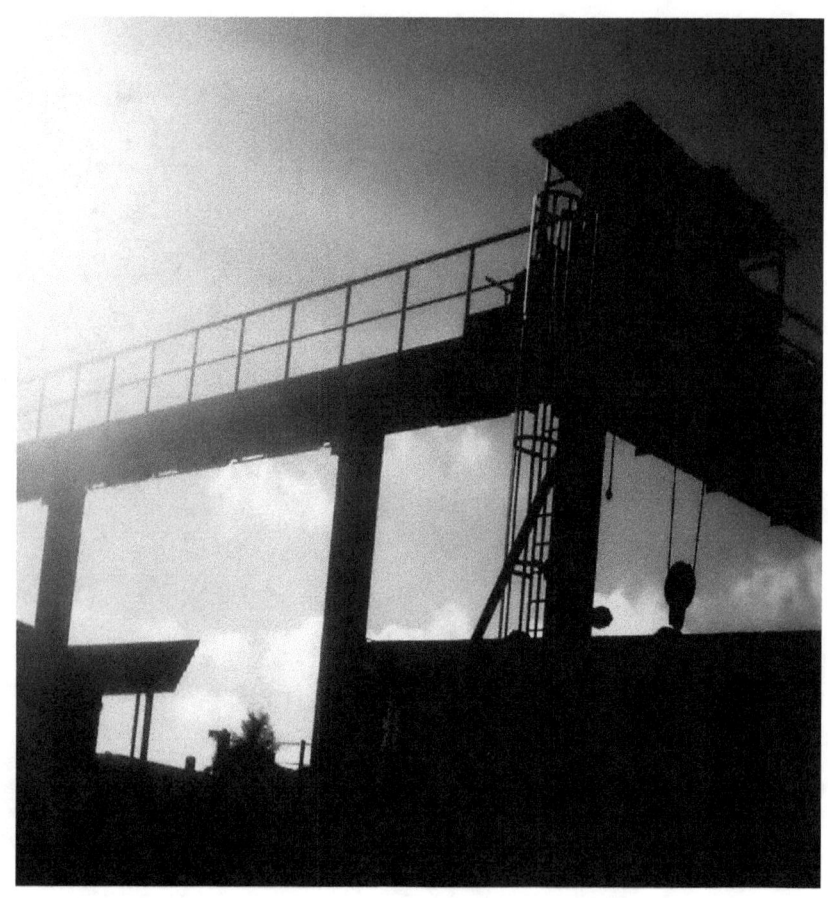

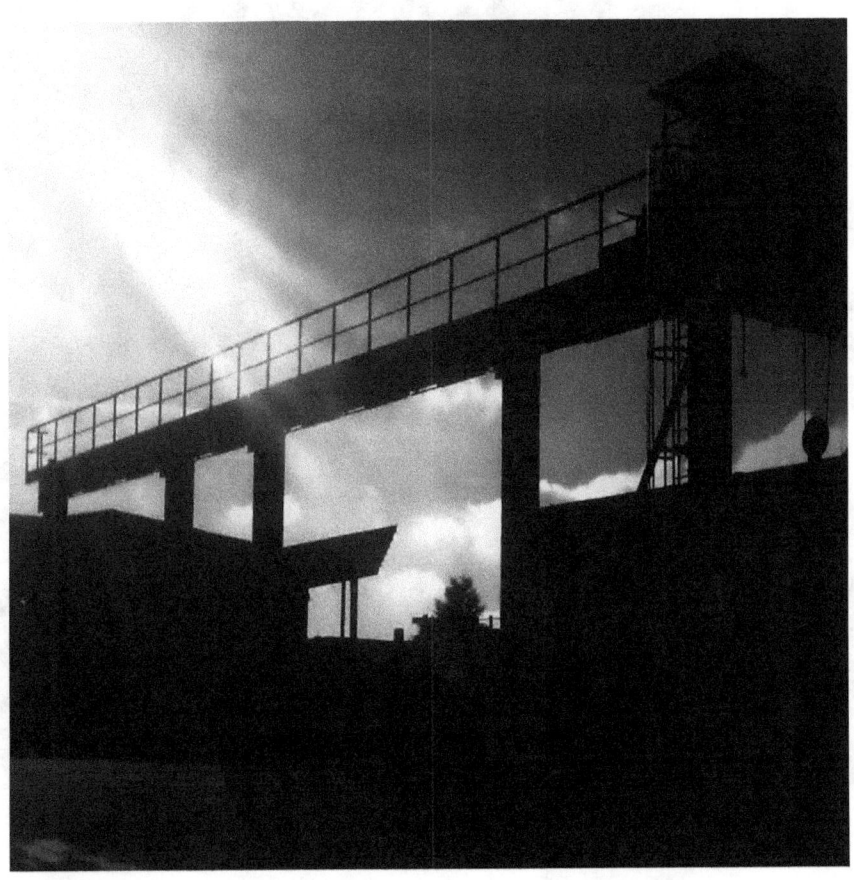

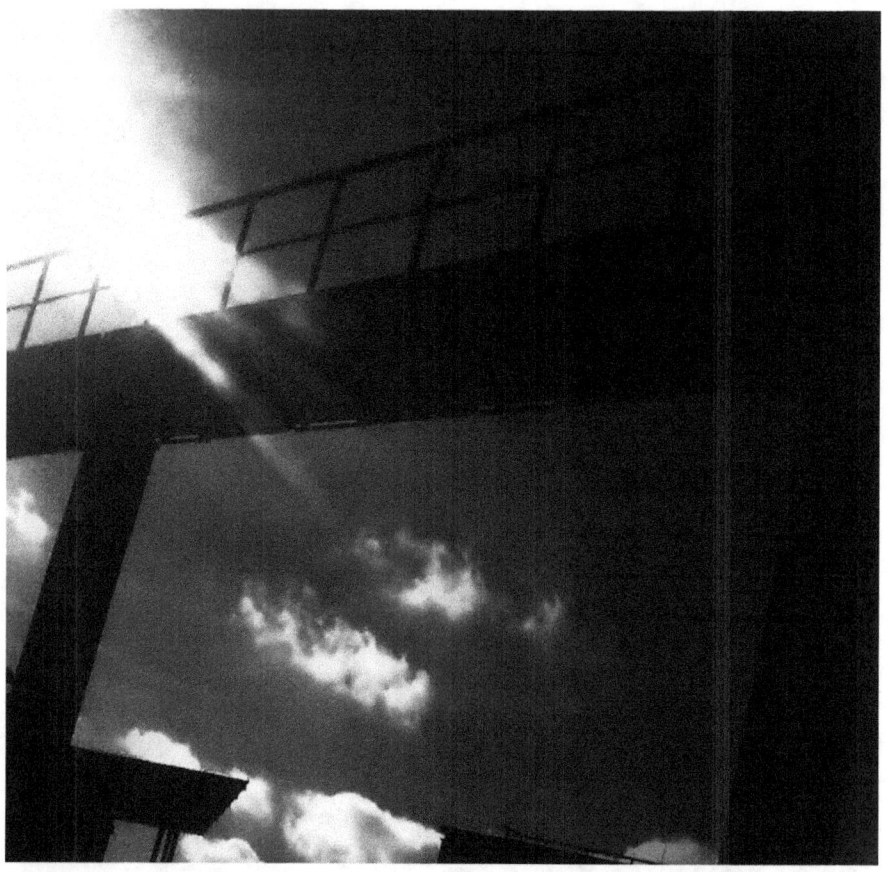

Simone Kaplan											Black & White: Abstract

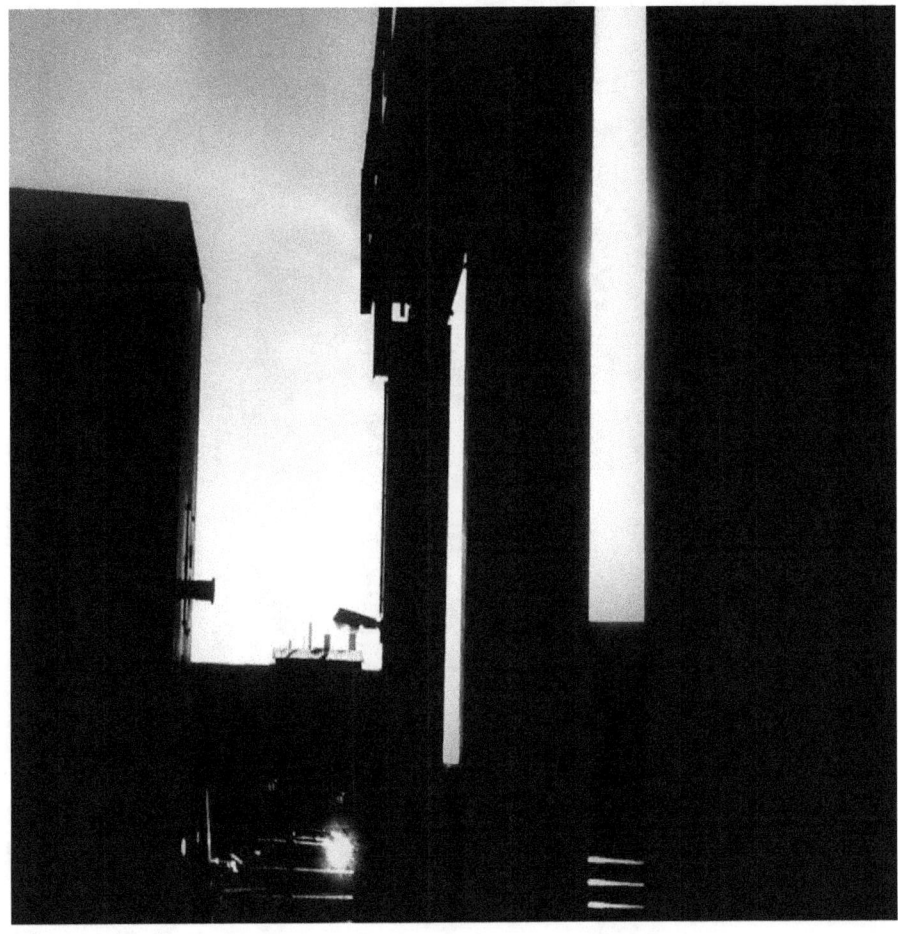

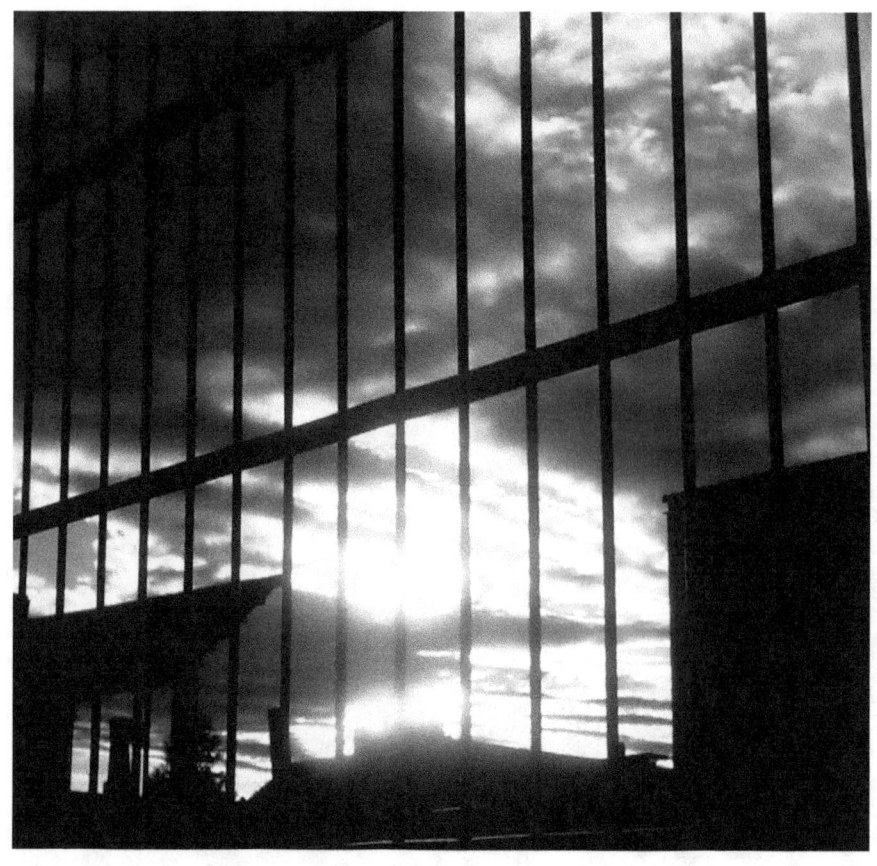

Simone Kaplan   Black & White: Abstract

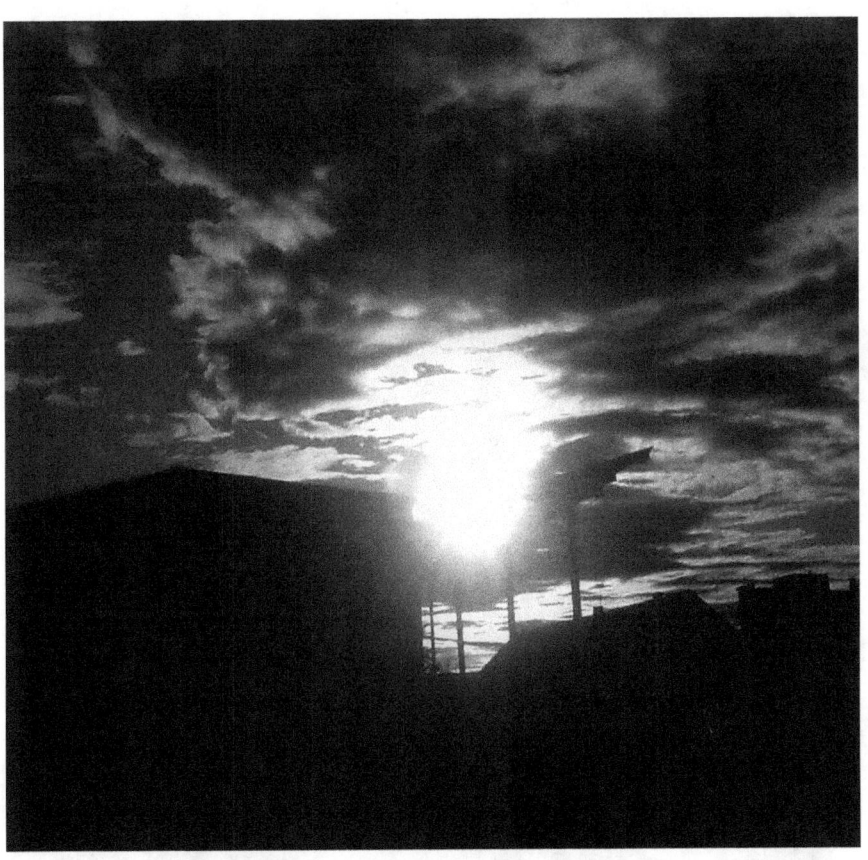

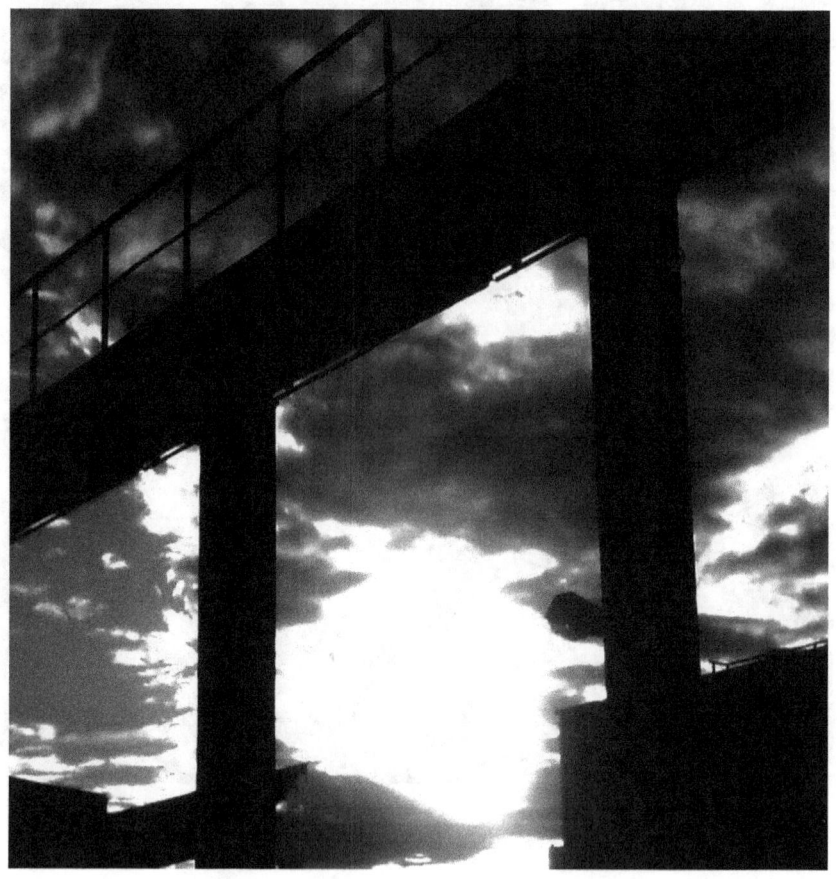

Simone Kaplan							Black & White: Abstract

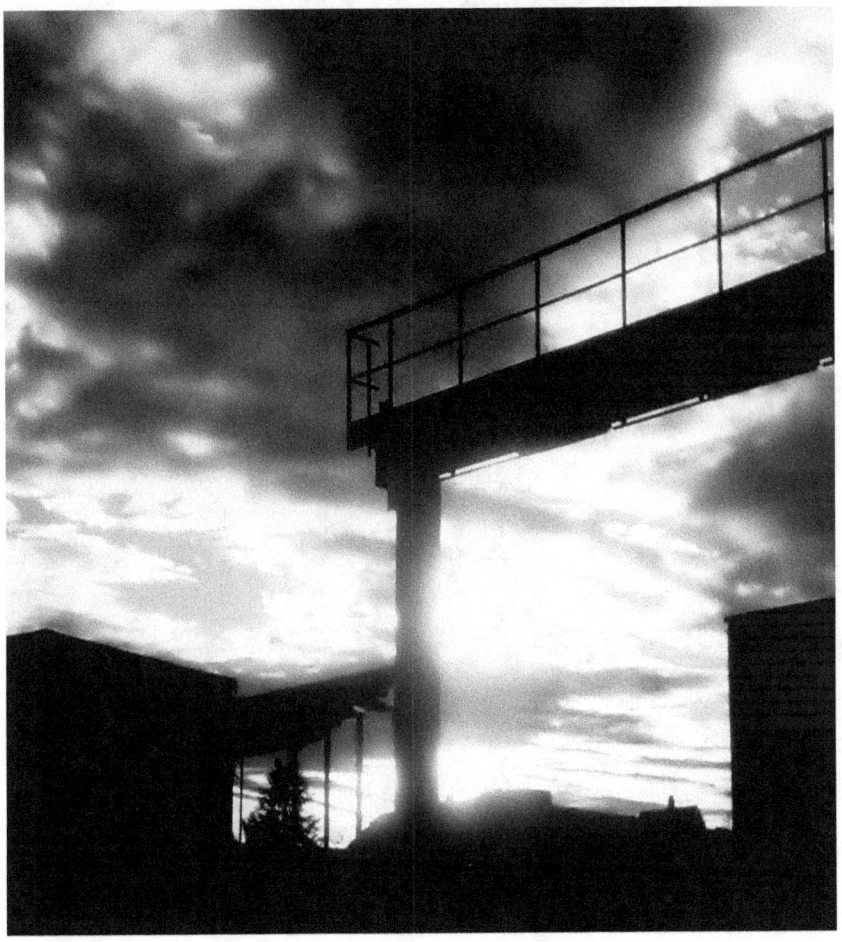

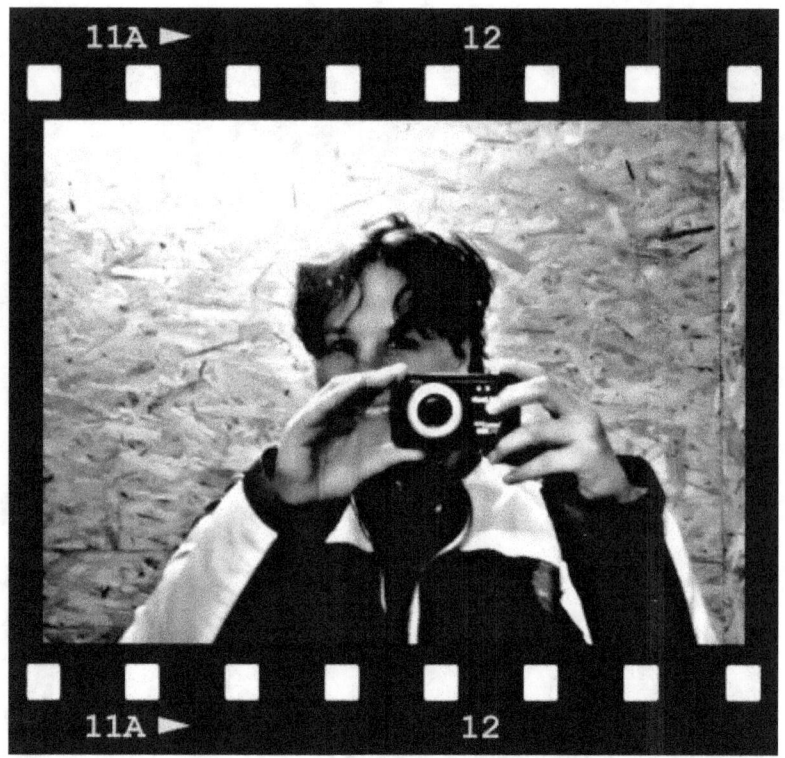

Simone Kaplan

Thank you for your visit.

THE END

www.ingramcontent.com/pod-product-compliance
Lightning Source LLC
Chambersburg PA
CBHW071747170526
45167CB00003B/973